CONSIDERING JESUS

Studies in the Book of Hebrews

Andrew D. Erwin

ISBN: 978-1-960858-11-5

Published by:

Cobb Publishing
704 E. Main St.
Charleston, AR 72933

(479) 747-8372
www.CobbPublishing.com
Editor@CobbPublishing.com

To the students I have taught in schools of preaching and Bible colleges this volume is humbly dedicated.

"But, beloved, we are confident of better things concerning you yes, things that accompany salvation" (Hebrews 6:9).

Abbreviations

DSS – Dead Sea Scrolls

ESV – English Standard Version

KJV – King James Version

LXX – Septuagint

NASB – New American Standard Bible

NIV – New International Version

NKJV – New King James Version

NT – New Testament

OT – Old Testament

Contents

Introduction to Hebrews 7

Section One 43

Section Two 69

Section Three................................. 95

Section Four.................. 145

Section Five.................. 175

Section Six... 225

Section Seven 237

Bibliography.. 239

Introduction to Hebrews

The significance of the epistle to the Hebrews cannot be overstated for Christians. A.T. Robertson considered it as "the first great apologetic for Christianity" (as did A.B. Bruce), and in his estimation it "has never been surpassed."[1] Hebrews teaches the Christian about the distinctive nature of Christ's new covenant like no other document in the New Testament. While other NT documents treat the distinction between the covenants (e.g., Romans and Galatians), no other book in the canon comments as directly and extensively upon Christ's new covenant as does Hebrews.

> "Of all the precious writings that speak of the Christian faith, it is doubtful if any makes a more distinctive contribution than the Epistle to the Hebrews. It describes in an elevated, incomparable way the true nature and value of the Christian religion. For the author of the Epistle, Christianity is the *better* and *best* of all possible religions. Beside it, there is no other."[2]

---

[1] A.T. Robertson, *The Epistle to the Hebrews* in Word Pictures in the New Testament, vol. 5 (Nashville, TN: Sunday School Board of the Southern Baptist Convention, 1932), 331.

[2] Neil R. Lightfoot, *Jesus Christ Today: A Commentary on the Book of Hebrews* (Abilene, TX: Bible Guides, 2001), 19.

Christ is presented as our Apostle, Priest, and King. As our Apostle, Christ is superior to the prophets and to the angels (1:4-2:18) who, as ministers of God, were often used to convey God's message to Israel. As a lawgiver, Christ is presented as being superior to Moses (3:1-19). As a leader over the people of God, Christ and His providential rest are superior to that granted through Joshua (4:1-11). As a Priest, Christ's Priesthood is superior to the Levitical priesthood (4:14ff; 7:1ff). His sin offering of His own blood is presented as superior to all other sacrifices offered by the priests of Israel (9:1ff). As King, Christ has been coroneted by His Father, as the Father has said to the Son, "Your throne, O God, is forever and ever; a scepter of righteousness is the scepter of Your kingdom" (1:8). Christians have received an unshakable kingdom (12:28), as was foretold by God through Daniel the prophet (Dan 2:44).

We find the appeal to "consider Jesus" being made twice in the epistle (3:1; 12:3). As one studies Hebrews, it can readily be observed that this is the message the writer desired to convey most of all. *Consider Jesus*. Evidence from within the book suggests that these were Christians who were being tempted to forsake Christ (3:12-13; 10:26-31, 35-39). With discouraged spirits, through various trials and longing eyes for their Hebrew heritage, the readers were considering leaving the Lord to return to Judaism. The exhortation to consider Jesus was a necessary message at a critical juncture in their lives.

The author's use of OT themes, and the conclusions drawn by such subjects, provide us with ample reason to believe these were Jewish converts to Christianity. Evidence also suggests these brethren were not maturing the way they should have matured in the faith (5:12-14). Some of them were forsaking the assembly of the church (10:25). They were warned not to "become sluggish, but imitate those who through faith and patience inherit the promises" (6:12). The recipients were encouraged to remain faithful and not draw back to perdition, but to believe unto the saving of their souls (10:39).

Despite the majesty of Hebrews, it is perhaps as well known for the difficulties it presents as it is for its distinctive contributions to our understanding of the covenant, ministry, and religion Christ. From the second century until now, the epistle of Hebrews has been the subject of debate. It is the only truly anonymous letter in the New Testament and is probably the most enigmatic book in the New Testament in terms of provenance.[3]

Hebrews also differs from most of the New Testament epistles in that it begins like a sermon, reads like a sermon, but includes a postscript like an epistle. Yet, even near its ending, the document is referred to as a "word of exhortation" (13:22).

The phrase "word of exhortation" also occurs in Acts 13:15 when Paul and Barnabas were invited to speak in the synagogue of Antioch of Pisidia. The use of the phrase in these passages has caused some modern scholars to conclude that it is an "idiomatic, fixed expression for a sermon in Jewish-Hellenistic and early Christian circles."[4]

We find no customary opening salutation containing the names of the writer or the people addressed. The writer warns and exhorts his readers in a very sermonic way, often using imperatives and hortatory subjunctives, e.g., "let us."

---

[3] David L. Allen, *Hebrews* in the New American Commentary, vol. 35 (Nashville, TN: B&H, 2010), 23-24.

[4] William L. Lane, *Hebrews 1-8* in the Word Bible Commentary (Dallas: TX: Word, 1991), lxx.

For this reason, we will be considering Hebrews as a "sermonic epistle" or even as an example of an early inspired sermon of the first century church.

The goal of the writer was one of exhortation, while he employed the means of exposition.[5] The first recipients would have received the epistle as an exhortation to remember their previous faithfulness and return to their former state.

While the forsaking of Christ might have appeared on the surface like a solution to their problems, it was by no means the answer. Their "quick fix" would have led to their ultimate destruction.

Recipients

Who first received the letter? Where did they live? When did they live? While we may not be able to answer these questions as definitively as we would like, "judging by the specificity of the warnings and moral exhortations that punctuate the document, the writer had specific readers in mind (see 5:12; 6:10; 10:32)."[6] The recipients of the epistle were

---

[5] Jon C. Laansma, "The Book of Hebrews," *The Dictionary for Theological Interpretation of the Bible*, 274-281.

[6] D.A. Carson and Douglas J. Moo, *An Introduction to the New Testament*, (Grand Rapids, MI: Zondervan, 2005), 596.

undoubtedly Hebrew in ethnicity. In fact, the earliest known title given to the epistle is simply, "Πρὸς Εβραιους" – "to the Hebrews."[7]

Moreover, we find little to no evidence of any Gentile background in the letter. In fact, there is not a non-Jewish argument in Hebrews. The entirety of Hebrews' argument is grounded in the Hebrew Scriptures. Hebrews quotes from the OT some 35 times with quotations which are generally longer than those found in other NT documents.[8]

Such an epistle filled with analogies to Jewish beliefs would hardly have seemed fitting to a congregation comprised of Gentile Christians. The use of the Septuagint throughout the epistle, and the polished Greek with which it is written, also suggests that these were Hellenistic Jews who had converted to Christianity. However, these features could characterize the author more than the recipients.

Hebrews appears to have been written while the temple in Jerusalem was still standing (8:4; 10:11; 13:10, 11). The practices of the temple are spoken in the present tense, which

---

[7] In 𝔓⁴⁶, Codex Sinaiticus, Codex Vanticanus, and the Washington Manuscript

[8] David McClister, *A Commentary on Hebrews* (Temple Terrace, FL: Florida College, 2010), 45.

seems to indicate these practices were ongoing at the time of writing. However, the writer of Hebrews also speaks of the tabernacle of Moses in both the past and the present tenses (although the tabernacle could have been used to refer to the temple). Josephus also spoke of the temple in the present tense after it was destroyed. The Greek present tense has a different force than the English present tense. While the most likely date still seems to be before September, 70 AD, when the temple was destroyed by Titus, the latest the epistle could have been written would have been approximately 95 or 96 AD, as Clement of Rome cited from Hebrews in his letter to the Corinthians (*1 Clement*). This theory suggests the epistle would have been written during the reign of Domitian (90s AD), but this seems unlikely due to the lack of bloodshed mentioned by the author (12:4).

It also appears that some considerable amount of time had elapsed from the recipients' conversion to Christ until the reception of the epistle. These Christians had reached a point in time in which they should have been teachers (5:11ff.). They had a record for good works (6:10). It also appears that they had already endured one period of persecution (10:32ff.). We have no way of knowing for certain when they were converted, but it would have been after 30 AD when the church began (Acts 2).

Broadly speaking, we can reasonably accept that the epistle to the Hebrews was written between 30 and 70 AD. As we have inferred, it appears that these Christians had already overcome one period of persecution and were at that time facing a second period of persecution (see 10:32-36). At the time they would have received the letter, they were again enduring "chastening" and were being called to endure (10:36; 12:1-11; 13:3). They had faced persecution resulting in imprisonment and the plundering of their goods. However, their present persecution had not reached the extreme point of bloodshed (12:4).

Perhaps dreading the idea of enduring another period of persecution, they were tempted to forsake Christ (3:12-13). Perhaps they had reached a point of spiritual depression and discouragement and had thus stopped maturing in the faith (5:12-14; 6:12). This would explain the tone of the book and the need to "strengthen the hands which hang down, and the feeble knees" (12:12).

Where were Jewish Christians persecuted between 30 and 70 AD? We learn from the book of Acts that Christians were persecuted in Jerusalem and Judea from the beginning. According to Eusebius, the church in Jerusalem was entirely Jewish,[9] which would fit the ethnicity of the first recipients. However, it seems unlikely that they would have been as polished in the Greek language as was the writer of Hebrews (if Josephus is any indication). A question could also be raised as to their familiarity with the Septuagint. We would also think it reasonable to suggest that they would have received the letter in either Hebrew or Aramaic, although a case can be made for Greek being a predominant language among Palestinian Jews. Again, we must state that these characteristics may speak more to the writer than to the recipients.

The early persecution of the church in Palestine was also followed by a period of peace (Acts 9:31). However, Hebrews does not mention that the recipients of the letter suffered martyrdom during their first persecution (10:32ff.; 12:4). It is possible that Hebrews 12:4 is speaking of the second persecution which the church was facing. Thus, the writer would not be commenting on the bloodshed suffered during the first period of persecution, but the lack of bloodshed yet to be suffered during the second (present) period of

---

[9] Eusebius, *Ecclesiastical History*, 4.5.

persecution. Hebrews 13:7 may also imply the martyrdom of such leaders as Stephen and James. However, Hebrews 10:32-34 clearly speaks of the first period of persecution and makes no mention of martyrdom.

We know from Acts that the church in Palestine did suffer martyrdom during its first period of persecution. The theory that the first recipients were Jewish Christians in Palestine also depends on a second period of persecution rising after the return of Paul to Jerusalem following his third missionary journey (Acts 21).[10] We have no concrete evidence of such a persecution ever occurring.

The churches in Judea also received help from other (Gentile) churches and then dispersed these contributions to needy saints and to others (cf. 1 Corinthians 16; 2 Corinthians 8-9; Romans 15:25). Such would fit with the statement of commendation given to the first recipients of the epistle (6:10). However, it is also true that these churches were more on the receiving end than the giving end on these contributions. For these reasons, a Palestinian destination is difficult to reconcile without at least a few lingering doubts.

---

[10] McClister, *A Commentary on Hebrews*, 36-37.

A second possibility for answering who the original recipients might have been is that they lived in proximity to the city of Rome. The Roman historian Suetonius tells us that Emperor Claudius expelled the Jews from Rome because there was rioting over a man named Chrestus.[11] [12] The date for this expulsion is generally accepted as 49 AD. A case can also be made to include Jewish Christians in Claudius' decree. The theory suggests that the Jewish Christians were suffering persecution at the hands of non-believing Jews in Rome. Claudius decided to expel all the Jews, including Christians, from the city to restore peace. This would also help to explain why Aquila and Priscila left Rome (Acts 18:2). Accordingly, the persecution in Rome which led to the expulsion would be considered the first persecution suffered by the recipients of the letter. The second persecution is generally considered to be at the hands of Nero (64-68 AD).

During Nero's persecution, Christians were primarily persecuted in and around the city of Rome. While the early church may have been persecuted in various other cities to please Nero, they were never persecuted to the extreme that

---

[11] Suetonius, *Claudius*, 25:4.

[12] The Greek eta and iota were often used interchangeably due to similarities in pronunciation, as is also evidenced in Codex Sinaiticus which spells "Christian" with an "e" in Acts 11:26; 26:28; and 1 Pet 4:16.

they were persecuted in Rome. We also know from Paul's letter to the church at Rome that the church had both Gentile and Jewish Christians, making it entirely possible that the Jewish Christians in Rome were the first recipients of this letter. In fact, many signs seem to point to them. This church would have been around long enough to have the record indicated by the author (6:10). They would have felt the temptation to relieve their current sufferings and any admonition against such would apply. They were certainly familiar with the OT and any comparison made to it. And, being in Rome, their economy, freedom, and lives were at stake due to this persecution.

While persecutions varied throughout the empire prior to 70 AD, they did not occur outside of Palestine on any official basis until 64 AD. Early on, Christians were considered a sect of the Jews. Their religious freedom was protected by the same laws that protected the Jewish religion. Nero was the first emperor to enact laws specifically against Christians. Nero's persecution of the church did not begin until after the fire of July 18, 64 AD swept through the city of Rome, destroying ten of the fourteen sections of the city. Two of the sections not destroyed were heavily populated by Jews and Christians. Once Nero began to be blamed for the fire by the citizens of Rome, he sought a scapegoat and found one in the Christians. Tacitus provides the earliest account of this persecution as well as the first Gentile record of the crucifixion of Christ.

"Therefore, to stop the rumor [that he had set Rome on fire], he [Emperor Nero] falsely charged with guilt, and punished with the most fearful tortures, the persons commonly called Christians, who were [generally] hated for their enormities. Christus, the founder of that name, was put to death as a criminal by Pontius Pilate, procurator of Judea, in the reign of Tiberius..."

"Accordingly, first those were arrested who confessed they were Christians; next on their information, a vast multitude were convicted, not so much on the charge of burning the city, as of 'hating the human race.'"

"In their very deaths they were made the subjects of sport: for they were covered with the hides of wild beasts, and worried to death by dogs, or nailed to crosses, or set fire to, and when the day waned, burned to serve for the evening lights. Nero offered his own garden players for the spectacle, and exhibited a Circensian game, indiscriminately mingling with the common people in the dress of a charioteer, or else standing in his chariot. For this cause a feeling of compassion arose towards the sufferers, though guilty and deserving of exemplary capital punishment, because they seemed not to be cut off for the public good but were victims of the ferocity of one man."[13]

It is generally believed that Paul's second imprisonment in Rome occurred during this time (possibly 65-66 AD, although a later date of 67-68 is plausible). Paul also stated that he "was delivered out of the mouth of the lion" (2 Timothy 4:17) during his second Roman imprisonment. Seeing that the church had "not yet resisted to bloodshed, striving against sin" (12:4), it seems that the date of writing would have had to have been before Paul was imprisoned and thus before or very early in Nero's persecution of the church, possibly between the trials and the executions of the Christian martyrs. Assuming this to be the case, the date of writing would likely be between 63-4 and sometime in 65 AD. This makes for a very tight window. It is possible that the author was somewhere close to the city of Rome (cf. 13:24), which would make for a shorter distance for the document to travel. It could be argued, however, that this does not leave enough

---

[13] Tacitus, *Annals of Imperial Rome*, 15.38-44.

time for the readers to become dull of hearing (5:11) and to begin forsaking the assembly (10:25).

One final theory which we shall discuss that could explain the identity of the first recipients concerns the churches in the region of Galatia. We know that Paul suffered persecution at the hands of disbelieving Jews in the region of Galatia on his first missionary journey (Acts 13-14). Paul also noted false teachers among them who sought to avoid persecution by instructing them to be circumcised (Galatians 6:12). Could it be that the writer of Hebrews was writing to Jewish Christians in this region? It is certainly possible. However, the same could be said for Christians in places like Thessalonica, Berea, and Corinth (Acts 17-18). Egypt (Alexandria) has also been suggested as a possible destination for the letter.

It is commonly believed that Hebrews was written to encourage Jewish Christians not to leave Christ and return to the Jewish religion. Jewish Christians would have considered a return to Judaism over any other religion or being non-religious. The epistle emphasizes the priesthood and sacrificial system of the OT, as is evidenced by a sizeable portion of the epistle being dedicated to these subjects. Why would the writer stress a comparison between Christ and the OT sacrificial system if a return to Judaism on the part of his readers was not at least a possibility? However, the primary issue these Christians faced was one of hardness of heart. They had become "dull of hearing." Renewed persecution, social marginalization, and a constant struggle with hardship and rejection appear to be the real issues facing these Christians.

The true essence of Christianity needed to be embraced by the readers. They were called to "consider Jesus" (3:1; 12:3) – His word, His ministry, His priesthood, His sacrifice, His suffering, His kingdom, and His glory. Without such understanding, they were in danger of developing a heart hardened by the deceitfulness of sin (3:12-13), crucifying Christ afresh (6:6), willful sin (10:26), trampling under their feet the Son of God, counting the blood of the covenant as unholy, despising the Spirit of grace (10:35), and drawing back unto destruction (10:39).

The writer of Hebrews desired to see his brethren grow in their faith, and not shrink back. Both issues of spiritual growth and the danger of apostasy are addressed throughout the letter. As a Christian grows in faith, he moves away from the danger of apostasy. But, if the Christian stops growing, he becomes at risk for apostasy. To draw nearer to God and increase in faith, these Christians needed to be reminded of the greatness of Christ. Hebrew Christians would have taken great pride in their heritage and Jewish religion. But as good as that may have been, the religion of Christ is better.

Christ has spoken a word superior to the one spoken by prophets and the angels. His covenant, law, priesthood, sacrifices, and rest are superior to everything found in the OT. If the Hebrew religion was something to be desired, the religion of Christ should have been desired more. Not only would such a message help to prevent apostasy for Jewish Christians, but it would also confirm the entirety of the OT message and God's eternal purpose. Truly, His works were finished from the foundation of the world (4:3). Christ is the fulfillment of the OT. He is the living embodiment of the OT. He is the reason we call the Old Testament "old" (8:13). He is the reason it became obsolete. He is the author of our faith (5:9). He is the ultimate purpose and fulfillment of God's spoken and written revelation to man. To reject Jesus is to reject the very reason for the writing of the OT and the existence of the Jewish nation in God's plan of redemption. Clearly this message would have resonated with Jewish Christians. Just as Jesus was called to obey the Father through sufferings (5:8-9), so too must they.

Authorship

Various authors have been suggested for Hebrews. Through the years examples of possible authors include Paul, Barnabas, Apollos, Luke, Priscilla and Aquila, Silas (Silvanus), Philip, Peter, Jude, Mary (the mother of Jesus), Epaphras, and Clement of Rome.[14] Some of these suggested authors amount to little more than wild guesses and can be discarded for lack of any real merit. Stephen has also been suggested as a possible author due to similarities between Hebrews and his sermon (Acts 7).[15] These similarities include: 1.) a similar attitude toward the Law of Moses; 2.) an emphasis on wandering as part of the life of the faithful; 3.) God's word is called "living"; 4.) references to Joshua and "rest" for God's people; 5.) references to the law being delivered through angels; and 6.) in the NT, only Stephen and the writer of Hebrews quote from Exodus 25:40.[16] However, it is highly doubtful that Stephen was alive when Hebrews was written.

---

[14] Simon Kistemaker, "The Authorship of Hebrews," *Faith and Mission* 18 (2001): 57-69.

[15] L.D. Hurst, *The Epistle to the Hebrews: Its Background of Thought* (SNTS Monograph Series 65; Cambridge, 2005), 94-106.

[16] McClister, *Hebrews*, 15.

Much of what has been suggested about possible authors is little more than conjecture. For example, Clement of Alexandria believed Paul was the author. He believed that Paul did not prefix his name to Hebrews, as was characteristic of Paul (cf. 2 Thessalonians 3:17), due to prejudice and suspicion on the part of the Jews toward him. He also believed that Paul did not want to appear to be the apostle sent to the Hebrews, since the Lord Himself was the "apostle of the Almighty" sent to the Jews.[17] Difficulties, however, arise from the assertions made by Clement of Alexandria. In the first place, Paul did not allow animosity to prevent him from identifying himself when writing to the Corinthians even though they had been exposed to false apostles who denied his apostleship and propagated a certain amount of hostility against him (cf. 1 Corinthians 9:1ff.; 2 Corinthians 10:10ff.). Besides that, whoever wrote Hebrews appears to have been on friendly terms with its recipients (see Hebrews 13:18-25).

Paul not attaching his name out of respect for the Lord is also merely a conjecture. Paul attached his name to his other epistles written to churches which included Jewish converts to Christianity. He did not fear being disrespectful in those

---

[17] Eusebius, *Ecclesiastical History*. 6.14.

letters. Why would he fear the appearance of being disrespectful to the Lord in this epistle? Moreover, if he was writing by the inspiration of the Holy Spirit and issuing a divine decree to hold fast to the faith, such a thought of being disrespectful to Christ would have scarcely entered his mind. Clearly, the writer of Hebrews was honoring Christ from the document's beginning to its ending. Attaching a name would have done nothing to diminish this fact.

If we consider Hebrews to be a sermon rather than an epistle, we might be able to explain why there is not a formal greeting as with Paul's epistles. If this is the case, Hebrews would simply not have been written like an epistle but like a sermon and would be an altogether different genre of inspired literature. When reading Hebrews, it can be quickly deduced that it is not an epistle. No names of acquaintances or co-workers are mentioned. No congregation or destination is mentioned. It has a sermonic flow. It is called a "word of exhortation" (13:22), and not an epistle in its conclusion. Is this reason enough to explain why Paul did not include his name, at least in the conclusion? Possibly. The arguments are Pauline in nature. Many of the illustrations given are found in Paul's other writings. The use of the subjunctive "let us" is common to Paul. The writer appears to have been in prison at some point and desired to be restored to them as was Paul. He was also a close associate of Timothy and had been in Italy (13:23, 24). A stronger case can be made for Paul as the author than for any of the other people suggested throughout history. In fact, there has never been a time when Paul was not considered to be the author by credible sources. Yet, from a very early time, some have treated Hebrews as Paul's and others have not. Nothing has changed regarding the question of Pauline authorship.

While we cannot state for certain that Paul was the author, we can state with confidence that the author was male. For, "The one place in the epistle where the requirements of Greek grammatical gender indicate the author's sex uses the masculine (11:32). The author says 'the time will fail me telling (διηγουμενον)...'"[18]

Not only was the author male, but he also appears to be Jewish. While it is not impossible that the author was Gentile, it is more likely that he was Hebrew. Those who would adopt the theory of Lucan authorship will no doubt have to wrestle with the fact that Luke was most likely a Gentile.[19]

---

[18] F.F. Bruce, *The Epistle to the Hebrews* (Grand Rapids, MI: Eerdmans, 1977), xl.
[19] In Colossians 4:11 and 14, Luke is not listed among those who were "from the circumcision."

Another indication that the author was Hebrew is his pause to explain a Hebrew name (7:2). He appears to have quoted often from the LXX.[20] It is believed that the writer's Greek is also more elegant, polished, and smoother than the known letters of Paul.[21] In fact, Hebrews is generally acknowledged to be written with the best Greek in the NT.[22] The writer of Hebrews also offers very direct and explicit argumentation which indicates that he was schooled in rhetoric.

For these reasons, many scholars believe the author could have been Apollos, who was an Alexandrian, Hellenistic Jew (cf. Acts 18:24ff). Martin Luther held this view. However, if Apollos was the author, why did a fellow Alexandrian in Clement believe the author to be Paul? This may not be enough to discount the possibility of Apollos as the author entirely, but it is a question deserving an answer.

Was the author an eyewitness or apostle? Did he receive the word directly from the Lord or through the preaching of

---

[20] While some scholars have suggested that the writer was also quoting from the DSS, there is no evidence from within the epistle to affirm that he or the original recipients were members of any fringe group of Judaism. In fact, the case appears to be quite the opposite as Hebrews contains very orthodox views for first century Judaism.

[21] A.T. Robertson, *A Grammar of the Greek New Testament in the Light of Historical Research* (Nashville, TN: Broadman, 1934), 132-33.

[22] Andrew H. Trotter, Jr., *Interpreting the Epistle to the Hebrews* in *Guides to New Testament Exegesis* vol. 6 (Grand Rapids, MI: Baker, 1997).

those that heard Him (2:3)? Or is the author speaking rhetorically? Barnabas would be a likely candidate for authorship. He was a great encourager and a Levite (cf. Acts 4:36). Clearly, such a "word of exhortation" (13:22) and call for encouragement (10:24; 13:1; 13:21) would have been characteristic of him. Being a Levite, the discourse on the priesthood of Christ would certainly seem to be another characteristic of Barnabas. He was also a respected leader in the early church (Acts 14:14).

The author appears to have been among the recipients (or possibly one of them) at one time by soliciting their prayers that he may be "restored" to them sooner (13:19). The basic meaning here is "to restore to an earlier condition." The author was as "a man at a distance from his friends and [desired] to be restored to them."[23] If the recipients were from Rome, then it appears that the author would have at least had to have visited Rome at some time for some considerable duration. The same would hold true for a Palestinian or Galatian destination. In this case, Paul, Luke, Barnabas, and Apollos would all fit as possible authors. However, Luke was not a Jew and it seems unlikely that a non-Jew would

---

[23] Joseph H. Thayer, *Thayer's Greek-English Lexicon of the New Testament* (Peabody, MA: Hendrickson, 2002), 62.

have written this letter. As for Barnabas and Apollos, we do not have enough evidence pertaining to their travels among the churches to say for certain that it was one of them. Paul seems to be the most likely candidate for authorship, and we have no valid reason to doubt it. Yet, we must admit as Origen has well-said, "As to who wrote the epistle, truly only God knows."[24] For this reason, we shall refer to the author of Hebrews simply as "the writer" throughout our study.

To summarize, it appears that Hebrews was written to Jewish Christians between 49 and 70 AD, and most likely in the early to mid-60s. They could have lived in one of at least three possible regions – Rome, Galatia, or Palestine. The author was likely a Jew who was taught by an apostle or was an apostle. The most likely possibilities include Paul, Apollos, and Barnabas, with Luke being discounted for not being Jewish.

The message was a word of exhortation not to forsake the Lord, but to consider Jesus amid trials, draw strength from Him, and endure whatever sufferings may come. To surrender faith in Christ meant to surrender all hope (6:18-19).

---

[24] Eusebius, *Ecclesiastical History*, 6.14.

Canonicity

For several years after the close of the NT period, the canonical status of the book of Hebrews was a legitimate concern, especially among the churches in the West. The Muratorian Canon (circa 170-180) excludes it. In the East, Hebrews was accepted as Pauline from the second century onward.[25] In fact, the Syrian "fathers" never disputed its canonical status.[26]

The reason for some speculation about the epistle in the West seems to be its misuse by certain heretical groups in that region. Hebrews 6:4-6 was especially distorted by Montanus and Novatian, who rejected postbaptismal repentance by those who recanted their faith when confronted with persecution.[27] By the fourth century, the Council of Hippo (393) and the Council of Carthage (397) recognized Hebrews as canonical, owing to the influence of Jerome and Augustine.[28]

---

[25] Harold W. Attridge, "Epistle to the Hebrews," in vol. 3 of *Anchor Bible Dictionary*. Edited by David Noel Freedman (New York: Doubleday, 1992) 104.

[26] Carson and Moo, *Introduction*, 613.

[27] Simon Kistemaker, *Hebrews*, Baker New Testament Commentary (Grand Rapids, MI: Baker, 1984), 13.

[28] Carson and Moo, 613.

Textual Issues

Hebrews contains approximately 60 textual variants. However, of these 60 variants, none are what we would call thorny issues. Many of these variants simply differ on the use of the *nome sacrum* (sacred name) for the Father, Son, and Spirit, with most of the better manuscript evidence in favor of the sacred name. However, in Hebrews 4:12 the use of the *nome sacrum* renders a separation of the Holy Spirit and the human soul.[29]

In some passages, however, a variant reading may produce a better understanding of the author. For example, in 1:1 a variant exists between "the fathers" and "our fathers." If the text is best translated "our fathers" we would have even more reason to believe the author was a Jewish man writing to a Jewish audience.

A study of Hebrews 10:34 will also affect the way we consider the author. Was the author once "in chains" or was he alluding to "prisoners" supported by the recipients of the letter? The conclusion we draw rests on a single iota. The Critical Text (CT) uses δεσμιοις (prisoners) while the Textus

---

[29] Philip Comfort, *A Commentary on the Manuscripts and Text of the New Testament*, 371-82.

Receptus (TR) uses δεσμοις (chains). Unfortunately, there is strong manuscript evidence to support both renderings and it is difficult to reach a concrete conclusion from this verse alone. Metzger states his preference of δεσμιοις because of good representation from the Alexandrian, Western, and Eastern text types.[30] Philip Comfort is less certain, stating, "In the end, it is difficult to decide between the readings…"[31] However, the desire to be restored to them soon (13:19) could indicate a prior or current imprisonment for the author.

Another interesting passage to consider from Hebrews is 4:2. Herein, the TR follows some early versions to render the passage, "[the word] was not mixed with faith in those who heard it" (NKJV). The CT follows early papyrus documents and many other early manuscripts to render the passage, "they were not united by faith with those who listened" (ESV). One rendering leads us to believe the Israelites did not receive the word with faith. The other rendering leads us to believe that the Israelites, who heard the word through Moses, Joshua, Caleb, did not share their faith.

---

[30] Bruce Metzger, *A Textual Commentary on the Greek New Testament* (second edition; Germany: UBS, 1994), 600-601.

[31] Philip Comfort, *New Testament Text and Translation Commentary* (Carol Stream, IL: Tyndale, 2008), 711.

One final textual issue we shall note is the use of the word "unbelieving" over "disobedient" in 3:18; 4:6, 11; 11:31. The two ideas can be used interchangeably to speak of a person's sinful attitude (see 3:18-19). Thus, no major concerns come from the variant readings.

Theological Themes

Verbal inspiration is the first principle taught in the book of Hebrews. The writer not only acknowledged the verbal inspiration of the scriptures, but also the progressive nature of revelation, as God spoke at different times. After God revealed His will to man by men, He chose to speak through the revelation of His Son. By the same inspiration, those that heard Jesus taught these Jewish Christians (2:1-4). The writer affirmed that God's word remains living and active (4:12). The readers were not to refuse Him who speaks (12:25).

The sacrificial death of Jesus is also a central theological theme in the epistle to the Hebrews. The writer of Hebrews presented Jesus as both Son of God and Son of man. He is greater than the angels. Yet, He became lower than the angels to bring salvation to humanity. Christ became man so that He might taste death for every man (2:9).

The writer made clear that the new covenant became effectual because of Christ's death (9:15ff.). He reminded his Jewish readers of how things were sanctified by blood according to the first covenant. It was not until the blood was shed and applied that anything could be counted as clean. Just as that testament was enjoined by the shedding of blood, so too is this testament. Only His new covenant contains the promise, "I will remember their sins no more." In 8:18, the writer spoke of the "weakness and un-profitableness" of the law. In 9:7, he recognized that the law was not "faultless." He presented the chief weakness and fault of the law and its sacrificial system. Namely, it could not purify the conscience. There remained a remembrance of sins year after year (10:1). But, when Jesus offered Himself, He brought forgiveness of sins once and for all (10:12-14).

The writer also carefully considered Christ's relationship to the church. As Moses was indeed faithful in all of God's house (3:2), even as a servant (v.5), it is Christ who is the builder of the house (v.3), and has honor not only as the builder, but as the Son (v.6). Jesus is presented as the Apostle and High Priest of His church. Being the Apostle over the church, the readers were hear His voice (12:25). If they would continue listening, they could (1) hold confidence until the end; (2) keep their hearts from becoming hardened; and (3) enter His rest at the end of their sojourn. The writer wanted his readers to consider Jesus as One sent with a message which must be held fast from the beginning of their journey unto end.

The writer pointed out that if the children of Israel would have held fast to the word of Moses, they would not have perished in the wilderness. They would have entered the Promised Land. He then offered an analogy to heaven and to the crisis facing his readers. But, if they were to provoke God through their disobedience and unbelief, they would ultimately be aligned with all those who fell (3:18-19) and fail to reach the heavenly promised land.

As High Priest over His people, Jesus is interceding. The writer stated the duty of every priest was to serve as a mediator, standing between man and God offering both gifts and sacrifices for sins (5:1ff.). In so doing, the writer acknowledged Christ as their mediator several times throughout Hebrews.

Christ is recognized as King over His kingdom. He waves His scepter of righteousness (1:8). His kingdom is immovable (12:25ff.). As citizens of His kingdom, the readers were instructed to serve God with reverence and godly fear (12:28). This instruction seems to incorporate all the ethical warnings and instructions found in chapters twelve and thirteen.

The writer voices the Lord's displeasure and disappointment in them for their lack of spiritual maturity and their inability to understand the more difficult teachings of God's word (5:11ff.). The recipients had been given the time to become teachers and to understand the "meat" of the word. Yet, they were still in need of the first principles, to such a degree that they needed to be taught these things again. The recipients needed to learn how to discern good from evil. The writer urged his readers to get back to growing in their faith, lest they should become hardened in their heart to a point of no return (6:4-6).

The possibility of apostasy was a primary concern for the writer, and he wanted it to be a primary concern for his readers. He did not want them to fail. God remembered their good work and loved them for it (6:10). Upon reminding them, the writer encouraged them not to be sluggish. He offered encouragement in the examples past figures as a means of provoking love and good works (6:12)

The writer wanted his readers to trust in the promises and certainty of God's word. Two immutable things are stated for their consideration: God's promise and His oath. God cannot lie. Because of God's righteousness the readers had a strong consolation and a refuge of hope.

In 10:26ff., the force of the writer's language is clear as he warned his readers about willful sin. If the readers were to continue in willful sin, the blood of Christ would no longer remain as a source of cleansing and forgiveness. In this case, they would have rejected His offering, trampled His blood beneath their feet, and forsaken all blessings found in Him. Heaven would no longer await them, but only a certain fearful expectation of the judgment and of the fiery indignation which shall consume all of the adversaries of God.

The writer concluded this line of reasoning by bringing to their attention the very nature of God. God demands retribution for sins. He has paid that sin debt by giving His Son. If they were to choose to turn back from His sin offering, then they would pay the personal retribution and punishment owed. God will repay for the iniquity of the wicked (10:30). Unfortunately, many evangelical scholars are unwilling to allow for the possibility of apostasy among Christians. Some have even denied that the first recipients of the letter were even saved.[32] The assertion that these first recipients were not saved can be answered by acknowledging that the author included himself in his warnings (see 10:26). Moreover, his and their sins had been purged (1:3). Furthermore, it is against the grain of Hebrews to speak of salvation in purely eschatological terms. The writer understood that grace and mercy could be enjoyed in this life (4:16).

To overcome their trials and remain faithful, the readers would have to follow the faithful example of certain OT heroes (11:1ff.), the Lord Himself (12:3); and their faithful church leaders (13:7). These readers had a need for endurance. Their persecution had not yet reached its most severe climax, the shedding of blood (12:4). A vivid picture of a wearied runner straightening up and gaining his second wind is presented in 12:12-13. This is what the recipients needed to do. They were fainting. They needed to catch their wind,

---

[32] See Thomas R. Schreiner and Ardel B. Caneday, *The Race Set Before Us: A Biblical Theology of Perseverance and Assurance* (Downers Grove, IL: Inter Varsity Press, 2001), 193—204 and Frank Thielman, *Theology of the New Testament: A Canonical and Synthetic Approach* (Grand Rapids, MI: Zondervan, 2005), 606-607.

straighten up their posture and path, and finish the race. The persecution would pass, and if they remained faithful, they would receive the reward.

Outline of Hebrews

A. The Father Speaks through the Son, 1:1-3.
  (1) God has spoken to the fathers throughout history, 1:1.
  (2) God is speaking in these last days through His Son, 1:2a.
  (3) The Credentials of Christ, 1:2b-3.
B. The Superiority of Christ to the Angels, 1:4-2:18.
  (1) In Name, Relationship, Deity, Honor, and Work, 1:5-14.
  (2) The More Earnest Heed Given to His Word, 2:1-4.
  (3) The Reason for Christ becoming Human, 2:5-18.
C. The Superiority of the Son to Moses and Joshua, chs. 3 and 4.
  (1) The Superiority of Christ to Moses, 3:1-6.
  (2) The Failure of Israel under Moses and Joshua, 3:7-4:2.
  (3) The Proofs that the Rest is Still Available, 4:3-10.
  (4) The Need of Striving to Enter this Rest, 4:11-13.
  (5) The Triumph of Christ, our High Priest, an Incentive to Drawing Near, 4:14-16.
D. The Nature and Scope of Christ's High Priesthood, chs. 5-7.
  (1) The Qualifications of Christ as High-Priest, 5:1-10.
  (2) Spiritual Understanding and Growth, 5:11-6:20.

(3) The High-Priesthood of Christ Prefigured by Melchizedek, 7:1-25.

(4) The High-Priesthood of Christ Contrasted with the Levitical Priesthood, 7:26-28.

E. The Ministry of Christ as High Priest, 8:1-10:18.

(1) The Circumstances of His High-Priestly Ministry, ch. 8.

(2) The Sanctuary and Service under the Two Covenants, ch. 9.

(3) The Contrast between the Levitical Sacrifices and the Sacrifice of Christ, 10:1-18.

F. The Application of the Truths Discussed, 10:19-12:29.

(1) The Exhortations to Faithfulness Under the New Covenant, 10:19-39.

(2) Encouragement from the Faith of Others, 11:1-12:4.

(3) The Relationship of Sonship to the Father, 12:5-13.

(4) A Warning Against Failure and Apostasy, 12:14-17.

(5) The Greater Proposition for the Christian, 12:18-29.

G. The Christian and Life's Relationships, 13:1-19

(1) To Brethren, 13:1.

(2) To Strangers, 13:2.

(3) To Prisoners, 13:3.

(4) To a Spouse, 13:4.

(5) To God, 13:5-6.

(6) To Shepherds in the Church, 13:7, 17

(7) To Dietary Laws, Altars, and Christ, 13:8-16.

(8) Prayer Request, 13:18-19.

H. Conclusion, 13:18-21.

(1) Blessings to the Recipients, 13:20-21.

(2) Postscript, 13:22-25

Conclusion

Hebrews provides everything a Bible student should desire in a study. The book will take you into a study of church history and theology. If you are a minister, you have an abundance of homiletic passages to analyze. If you are a textual critic and like to exegete passages, you can see how the different NT manuscripts build from each other while engaging in interesting word studies.

Most importantly, if you are a Christian who is discouraged and are experiencing a period of spiritual depression, even teetering on the point of apostasy, Hebrews will provide you with words of encouragement and warning. The writer of Hebrews will strike the modern student as being someone who truly believed that to lose heaven is to lose everything. God used this man to provide Christians of every age with a truly unparalleled apologetic for faith and an exhortation to greater faithfulness.

Section One

Christ Is Greater than the Angels

1:1 – 2:18

"God, who at various times and in various ways spoke in time past to the fathers by the prophets…" (1:1). The Hebrew homily begins with a statement of fact. The writer offers no introduction customary to epistles, no word of commendation for himself or the recipients, and no formal greeting. Without hesitation, reservation, or doubt, the writer announces the existence of God and the verbal inspiration of the scriptures He provided. God has revealed Himself to man through words. God has spoken. With unwavering simplicity and emboldened assurance that God exists, He has spoken, and His Son is Jesus Christ, the writer brings assurance and confidence to the heart of every believer.

That God would communicate to man through the medium of words and language should be obvious. How else would God have communicated to man if not through human words and languages? Words were needed to teach mankind both in the long ago, as well as in "these last days." Words

were spoken by God to men (the prophets) who then recorded them through the means of writing under the guidance
of the Holy Spirit (to the/our fathers). Thus, we have the inspired written word of God – the scriptures.[1] God spoke to
man in ages past by using prophets.[2] But in these last days,
His words have been spoken through His beloved Son.[3] The
writer wastes no time in placing before the reader a proper
consideration of Jesus. God spoke through prophets. Yet no
prophet could claim to be His Son. That honor belongs only
to Jesus.

God spoke *at various times*. The revelation of God's will
to man was given gradually. His word was not entirely revealed at one setting, but rather over a period greater than
1,000 years from Moses to Malachi. The gradual revelation
of His will served as a continual guardian and guide to bring
Israel to faith in Christ (Galatians 3:24). God spoke to the
prophets when He deemed the occasion necessary for the
communication of His will. He did so with great brevity, offering only the words He regarded as essential to the con-
veyance of His will according to His infinite wisdom.

---

[1] cf. 1 Corinthians 2:6-16; 2 Timothy 3:16-17; 1 Peter 1:10-12; 2 Peter 1:19-
21
[2] e.g., Jeremiah 1:9ff; Ezekiel 2-3; Daniel 2:19ff
[3] cf. John 8:12ff; 12:44-50; 14:10, 24, 31; 17:8, 14

God spoke *in various ways*. He spoke historically and prophetically. He spoke by psalms and proverbs. He pleaded with forthright messages intending to stir the human spirit to obedience. God gave both words of comfort and warning, "precept upon precept, precept upon precept; line upon line, line upon line; here a little and there a little" (Isaiah 28:10). The diverse nature of God's revelation is seen throughout the OT. God allowed His plans to be known and spoken via predictive prophecy using inspired prophets (Amos 3:7). God spoke amidst storms and thunder to Moses (Exodus 19:19; Deuteronomy 5:22). He spoke in a "low whisper" to the prophet Elijah (1 Kings 19:12). Our Father also revealed His will to a variety of individuals in their dreams (Genesis 40:8; 41:16; Daniel 2:19-23).

"In these last days He has spoken to us by His Son" **(1:2).** After God revealed His will to man in various ways through various people, He chose to speak to mankind through His Son. Jesus is the pinnacle, embodiment, and fulfillment of God's revelation to man. All other words, ways, and means of divine revelation have led to and point to Jesus as the Savior of the world.

God has "from the foundation of the world" (Matthew 25:34) revealed His plan to reconcile man and to save him from his rebellious ways. He has done so throughout the OT while looking back and ahead to the NT (see Isaiah 46:9-10; Ephesians 3:2-21). Jesus came to reveal the will of the Father through His preaching, by dying for the sin of the world, and in establishing His spiritual kingdom upon earth, thus inaugurating the last days.

The phrase *last days* (1:2) refers to the last dispensation, or the last period of world history. The periods of human history have included the patriarchal age from Adam to Mt. Sinai and the giving of the Law; the age of the law of Moses and the prophets, which extended until the Day of Pentecost; and now mankind is living in the age of the Messiah and His kingdom which began when the church was established on the Day of Pentecost (Acts 2).

The age of Christ will last until His return. The Christian Age is the accepted (chosen) time (2 Corinthians 6:2; Galatians 4:1-5) in which God has decided to reveal His eternal purpose to us by His Son and the holy apostles. God is not speaking to us merely by great and notable men as He once did. He is speaking to us by His Son, Christ Jesus, and this final age belongs to Him. We are now commissioned to do all that we do in the name of our Savior (Colossians 3:16).

The writer is by comparison emphasizing the authority of Christ by contrasting it to the authority of the prophets. If the prophets spoke with authority from God, how much more does His Son speak with authority. The premise of the superiority of Christ to the religious system He fulfilled will run as a golden thread throughout Hebrews. To accept the word of Christ is to accept the Father's offer of reconciliation and His eternal plan to save man.

The readers of this message must understand that if Christ be rejected, the only means of reconciliation with the Father is forfeited. Only Jesus can have the claim made of Him that He is appointed heir of all things; the creator of the world; the radiance and exact representation of the heavenly Father; the one who upholds the universe by His word; the one who grants purification through His blood; and the one who has sat down at the right hand of God (1:3). He is the embodiment of the scriptures He fulfilled. He is the Word made flesh (John 1:1-18). Where and to whom can man go to find what God has provided in Jesus? Truly Peter understood the gravity of turning from Christ when he said, "Lord, to whom shall we go? You have the words of eternal life. Also, we have come to believe and know that You are the Christ, the Son of the living God" (John 6:68-69).

In the first three verses of Hebrews, the writer says more about Christ and in fewer words than possibly any other passage in the Bible. Christ is "His Son, whom He has appointed heir of all things, through whom also He made the worlds; who being the brightness of His glory and the express image of His person, and upholding all things by the word of His power, when He had by Himself purged our sins, sat down at the right hand of the Majesty on high" (1:2-3).[4]

With startling brevity, the *mission* of Christ is summarized in revelation, creation, representation, and purification for our sins. In verses 4-14, the *majesty* of Christ will be analyzed through His name, relationship with the Father, dominion, power, and prominence.

A second proclamation begins in Hebrews 1:4 – **Christ is greater than the angels**. Not only is His authority greater than the prophets, but His nature and power are to be considered greater than the angels. The Jews of that day had an elaborate system of angelology. Angels were indeed referred to as "sons of God" many times in scripture. Perhaps they confused the "Son of God" with the "sons of God."

---

[4] cf. John 12:44-45; 2 Corinthians 4:4

"They came to think of angels as intermediaries be-tween God and man (and) also believed that there were millions and millions of them. They had many duties. They delivered messages, presided over the destiny of Israel, controlled the movement of stars, manipulated history. There were angels over the sea, the frost, the dew, the rain, the snow, the hail, the thunder and the lightning. There were angels who were wardens of hell and torturers of the damned. There were destroying an-gels and angels of punishment."[5]

The Holy Spirit deemed it necessary that these Hebrew Christians should be taken to the Hebrew scriptures and taught the superiority of the Messiah to the angels.[6] While comparing Christ to the angels the writer proves the follow-ing:

1.) Jesus has a more excellent name than any of the angels (v.4).

2.) Jesus has a greater relationship with the Father than do

---

[5] Robert L. Cargill, *Understanding the Book of Hebrews* (Nashville, TN: Broadman Press, 1967), 10
[6] In verse 5 the writer quotes Psalms 2:7 and 2 Samuel 7:14; verse six is de-rived from Deuteronomy 32:43; verse seven is taken from Psalms 104:4; verse eight is taken from Psalms 45:6,7; verse ten is from Psalms 102:25-27; and verse thirteen's source is Psalms 110:1.

the angels (vv.5, 6).

3.) The silence of the scriptures is authoritative.[7]

4.) The angels cannot be greater than Christ for they worship Him (v.6).[8]

5.) He is the creator of the angels (v.7).

6.) His is not just a son of God, He is God (vv.8, 9).

7.) He is eternal – without beginning or ending (vv.10-12).

8.) He sits at the right hand of God, exalted above any angel (v.13).

9.) Angels are ministering spirits, Jesus is God's Son (vv.5, 13, 14).

10.) Christ is Prophet (v.2), Priest (v.3), and King (vv.8-9, 13) – claims no man or angel could make and are not to be made about any man or angel.

"Today I have begotten You…" **(v.5).** This statement and the designation of Christ as "the firstborn" (v.6) may cause some unnecessary conclusions to be drawn concerning the

---

[7] "…to which of the angels did He say…" If God did not give the doctrine, man must not believe the doctrine (vv.5,13).

[8] Neither are angles to be worshipped (cf. Revelation 19:10).

divine nature of Christ. Some may conclude that He is a created being or that He is in a role of eternal sonship to the Father. However, these theories conflict with the immediate text under consideration and other pertinent passages relative to the discussion of the Deity of Christ.

Concerning the claim, "Today I have begotten You," James Burton Coffman wrote a reasonable explanation. He states with reference to Acts 13:33 and the second Psalm, "the begetting mentioned in this place is the resurrection of Christ. It was the resurrection that established all that Christ said and did, confirming the virgin birth, the incarnation, the miracles, the prophecies, everything."[9]

While it is true that Paul assigns meaning to Psalm 2:7 in Acts 13:33 with reference to Christ's resurrection from the dead, we cannot forget to consider Luke 1:35 in the discussion as well. Therein, we read that the Holy Child would be called the Son of God by virtue of being born through the power of the Most High. In John 1:14, the begotten-ness of Christ is associated with the Word becoming flesh. In scripture, Christ's being begotten of the Father can refer *both* to

---

[9] James Burton Coffman, *Commentary on Hebrews*, (Abilene, TX: ACU Press, 1971), 27

His birth and to His resurrection.

We find the statement from Psalm 2:7 again being made in Hebrews 5:5. The basis for the context of Hebrews 5:1-9 is the death and resurrection of Christ and the inauguration of His priesthood. When Psalm 2:7 is alluded to in these passages, the context is addressing the resurrection of Christ. No angel ever came in human flesh, died a human death, and was raised from the tomb by the power of God. No prophet, priest, or king ever died for the reconciliation of mankind. Only Jesus can be considered the begotten Son of the Father.

Jesus became the Son of God by virtue of the virgin birth and was declared the only begotten Son of God throughout His life. He is the "firstborn" regarding "the honor and dignity and primacy of Christ"[10] – in birth, in life, in death, and in eternity.[11] Jesus is the "firstborn over all creation" (Colossians 1:15); the "firstborn from the dead" (Colossians 1:18); and the firstborn in the church (Romans 8:29). The church is the assembly of the firstborn ones (12:23). Christ is the "first fruits" of the resurrection and all shall be raised from the grave just as He was raised (see 1 Corinthians 15:20-26; 44-

---

[10] Ibid.

[11] The term "firstborn" is sometimes used in the scriptures to denote divine favor. For instance, Rueben was literally the firstborn of Jacob (Genesis 35:23), but Ephraim was given that title in Jeremiah 31:9 as a sign of favor.

58).

No angel could claim to be begotten by the Father by means of a natural birth. No angel could claim to be begotten by God via a resurrection from the grave. By establishing these two points, the writer of Hebrews solidifies his case for the supremacy of Christ over the angels from his birth to His resurrection. Yet, he proceeds in ascending order to give even greater glory to the Son. The comparison of Christ to the angels would be incomplete without considering His deity. "Let all the angels of God worship Him" (v.6).[12] Exalted to the right hand of the throne of God, Christ rules with righteousness over His kingdom. Upon His ascension to the Father, the Father acknowledged Him and coronated Him, saying, ***"Thy throne, O God, is for ever and ever; A scepter of righteousness is the scepter of Thy kingdom."*** Your throne, Your scepter, Your kingdom, O God! Now, let all the angels of God worship Him!

"God, Your God has anointed you." Christ has been honored with a greater honor than any man or angel. He has been anointed as King by the Father over an eternal kingdom

---

[12] From Psalm 89:27

53

(Daniel 2:44ff.; Colossians 1:13; Hebrews 12:28). Just as Jesus honored the Father as God in life, the Father has honored Jesus as God in death. No angel has ever been invited to sit at the right hand of God. Not only is Christ recognized as the creator of the earth and the heavens,[13] He is attributed with eternality from Psalm 102:25-27. *"You remain, You are the same, Your years will not fail"* (vv.11, 12).

The heavens and the earth will perish, Christ will fold them up like a garment and they will be changed. His enemies will become His footstool, as even death and hell will be put in subjection to Him. Yet, He will remain. Contrasted to the eternality and unchanging nature of Christ is the temporary nature of His creation. Life on earth will not continue for eternity. Some believe that it will. Yet, the scriptures teach us that the world will come to an end at the return of Jesus. At this present time, Jesus rules over all heaven and earth. All authority has been given to Him by the Father (Matthew 28:18; 1 Corinthians 15:27). The government of His kingdom now rests upon His shoulders (Isaiah 9:6). When Jesus returns, He will gather the kingdom – those living and dead – and deliver it to the Father (Matthew 13:24-

---

[13] cf. John 1:1-3; Colossians 1:16

30; 36-43; 1 Corinthians 15:23-28).

The writer of Hebrews later affirms that Christ, "will appear a second time" (9:28). He is coming "Yet once more" (12:26). We are told only of a second coming of Christ, never more. Concerning His return, Paul wrote, "then comes the end" (1 Corinthians 15:23-24). The world will be destroyed at His coming (2 Peter 3:10-13). The only kingdom to be spared at His coming will be His kingdom (Hebrews 12:26-29). Christ's return signifies the end of this world (1 Corinthians 15:24). It will be the final event of this world.

The work of an angel is quite different from the work of the Son. Angels are God's ministers (v.7), even His *"ministering spirits sent forth to minister for those who will inherit salvation" (v.14)*. While Christ did come to minister and to give His life as a ransom (Mark 10:45), this was not and is not His only function. His ministry to man is not what makes Him divine in nature. Angels are heavenly agents of the providence of God. They vary in their functions according to the purpose of God. Angels are creatures. They are not eternal. They were created by God at some point prior to Genesis 1:1 (cf. Nehemiah 9:6; Psalm 148; Job 38:4-7). Christ was in the beginning, laying the foundation of the earth. The writer acknowledges, *"the heavens are the work of Your hands"* (v.7).

"Therefore, we must give the more earnest heed..." (2:1ff). The next chapter of Hebrews in the English Bible[14] is a continuation of the line of reasoning begun in chapter one. "Therefore" or "Because of this" we must give "the more earnest heed." Because of the greatness and supremacy of Christ as Son of God, as begotten of God, as Lord and God, we must give the more earnest heed to what He has said. Because of the work of Christ as Creator and Lord over creation, purging our sins, and as King over His spiritual kingdom, and the Father's ultimate messenger to man, we must give the more earnest heed to the things He has said. Everything the writer has been arguing has been leading the reader to this one point. *"How shall we escape if we neglect so great a salvation?"* (2:3). How is it possible for man to be saved if he rejects the one God has sent to save him?

As Hebrews continues, the reader will see time and again that Jesus is the only one who has, can, or will make a final offering for sin. He and His apostles have provided God's last word to man. Everything eternal hinges upon man's acceptance of Christ. Consider Jesus – "the author of eternal

---

[14] The earliest versions of Hebrews did not have verse and chapter divisions.

salvation to all who obey Him."

For these Hebrew converts to remain God's children and believe unto the saving of their souls (Hebrews 10:39), they would have to realize that their eternal fate depended upon their treatment of Christ and His gospel. They were going to be judged by Christ, His word, and their relationship to Him. To drift from His word would result in a departure from God's final and greatest revelation to man. To forsake Christ is to draw back unto perdition and expect nothing more than fiery indignation from God.

How shall we escape? If the OT was righteous and every transgression and act of disobedience was dealt with justly, how just might we consider the judgment that shall be against the disobedient one who forsakes the word of Christ? Man is free to choose and, therefore, God is just to punish. Such has always been the case. It is so now with man in his relationship with God. If this great salvation is indeed neglected by man, it will be by his doing. A person can live or die according to the teachings of Christ. Blessings or punishments will be rendered according to the person's decision. Notice the rhetorical "we" used by the writer. He is including himself in this word of exhortation. As a Christian speaking to other Christians, he asks, "How shall we escape if we neglect so great a salvation?

The great salvation is found only in Christ. It was first spoken by Him and was confirmed by those who heard Him. *"God was also bearing them witness,"* both with signs and wonders, and with various miracles, and gifts of the Holy Spirit, according to His own will.

The gospel was at first spoken by the Lord – referring to the personal ministry and preaching of Christ. It was confirmed by those that heard Him – speaking of the apostles (cf. 1 Corinthians 15:1-8). Through the outpouring of the Holy Spirit, the apostles were guided in their remembrance (John 14:26), judgment (John 16:8-12), and all truth (John 16:13). The apostles were guided to ensure the accuracy of the events they recorded (Luke 1:1-4) as the record they were writing was not from man but from God (1 Corinthians 2; 1 Peter 1:10-12; 2 Peter 1:19-21).

Through this outpouring of the Spirit on the apostles, they were enabled to bestow miraculous gifts to others and confirm the word they were preaching through miracles (Hebrews 2:1-4; Mark 16:17-20). The Father was bearing them witness through miraculous works and spiritual gifts. When divine revelation ceased, so too did the divine confirmation granted through miraculous gifts cease (cf. 1 Corinthians 13:8-13).

"For He has not put the world to come, of which we speak, in subjection to angels" (2:5). The KJV rendering of this passage is rather difficult to understand. Note, *"For unto the angels hath he not put in subjection the world to come, whereof we speak."* The NKJV offers an accurate translation which is easier to understand. When considering this statement, remember the previous comparisons which have been made concerning Christ and the angels. The Hebrew writer has been enlightening his readers as to why they should earnestly consider the word of Jesus, even over the word of angels. Christ is superior to them. While Christ has all authority, the angels are in subjection.

The phrase *"world to come"* is offered in connection to the previous thought found in 1:10-14. This world will perish (1:11; 12:27), but Christians have a greater hope in the world to come (6:5; 13:14).

"What is man...?" (2:6-8) The next passage begins by quoting Psalms 8:4-6. The Psalmist was certainly in awe of God's love for man. God is mindful of man. God does indeed remember, visit, and care for mankind. The readers could take great comfort in acknowledging the faithfulness of God. By using this passage from Psalms, the writer leads his readers to the point of Christ's birth. The writer also cites Psalms 8 to help us understand man's role in this world. The Psalmist reminds us of the dominion man was given over God's creation (cf. Genesis 1:26-28), a dominion that must be respected. While man has been placed over some things, he has not been placed over *everything* (2:8b).

"But we see Jesus..." **(2:9)** While we do not see man placed over everything, we do see (recognize) Jesus, who became man, suffered death for every man, and was crowned with glory and honor at His resurrection. The writer refers to Jesus' humanity as being "a little lower than the angels," just as he used the same term in referring to man. Why did Jesus become man? The remainder of chapter two answers that question.

He became a mortal man so that he might *"taste death for every man."* Herein we see the universality of the offer of reconciliation. Reconciliation is offered to every man, not some, not a predestined few, but to all. "He died to sin once for all" (Romans 6:10).

The NT teaches us who *can* be saved and who *will* be saved.[15] While Jesus died for every man, and every man could be saved, we know from Matthew 7:13-14 that many more will reject the offer than will accept it. Nevertheless, Jesus took on flesh to suffer death for everyone. Through Christ, God's grace is offered to man. In Christ alone are we are saved by God's grace (cf. Ephesians 2:1-8). He is the only "Savior of the world" (1 John 4:14).

"For it was fitting for Him…" **(2:10-13).** It is interesting to note the description of those who accept the offer of reconciliation in these few verses. They are called sons, sanctified, Christ's brethren, God's children, and the church. Jesus took on human nature, knowing He would suffer; yet, also knowing that through His suffering, He would establish such a relationship as this between God and man, thus making all spiritual blessings a reality for man through Him.

Also, observe again the writer's use of the OT. He relies on Psalms 22:22 and Isaiah 8:18 in this passage. He is using the OT to help his readers properly consider Jesus. He is proving by use of the OT that Christ, His covenant, and His

---

[15] Hebrews 2:9 is a passage that teaches who can be saved – every man. Compare this with Hebrews 5:8-9, which teaches us who will be saved – those that obey Him.

church were in God's plan from the beginning.

Moreover, consider the use of OT passages pertaining to the music of the church. We have here an account of a NT writer using an OT verse which alludes to singing. However, we never find a NT writer using an OT passage which includes instrumental music in worship. In passages speaking of worship and praise to God we read of the church or of individual Christians singing hymns in eight different passages.[16] Yet none of the Old Testament passages containing the use of mechanical instruments of music are cited in the New Testament. It stands to reason that had the use of instrumental music been desired by God for the church, that one of the inspired writers of the NT would have used a passage from the OT which included its use.

"Inasmuch then as the children have partaken of flesh and blood..." **(2:14-15).** Jesus became a partaker of flesh and blood to become "the same" as us. He did so to die a mortal death. Later in Hebrews, this concept will be explained in sacrificial terms. In this passage we read that He died (1) to destroy the devil and the power of death; (2) to deliver all of us who are subject to mortal death from the

---

[16] Romans 15:9, 11; 1 Corinthians 14:15, 26; Ephesians 5:19; Colossians 3:16; Hebrews 2:12; James 5:13

power of death.

Just as Jesus took on a physical body to become like us, in the resurrection, we will take on a spiritual body to become like Him. The spiritual body will be likened to Christ's glorious body, according to His holy working (Philippians 3:21; 1 John 3:2). The spiritual body will be eternal. "For we know that if our earthly house, this tent, is destroyed, we have a building from God, a house not made with hands, eternal in the heavens" (2 Corinthians 5:1). Flesh and blood cannot inherit the kingdom, and the perishable must be changed to imperishable (1 Corinthians 15:50). Man will bear a new image, the image of the heavenly (1 Corinthians 15:47-49). Thus, a new body will be given at the return of Christ and the resurrection of the dead (1 Corinthians 15:50-58).

"He does not give aid to angels..." (2:16). Jesus is not a mediator between God and angels, but between God and man (1 Timothy 2:5). He is the propitiation for our sins (1 John 2:1ff). Any angel who might have sinned is already condemned and without a Savior (Matthew 25:41; 2 Peter 2:4; Jude 6). To "give aid" can be literally translated as "to extend a helping hand." Christ "did not reach out a helping hand to angels, for He did not come to be their Savior, but

that of those who are descendants of Abraham by faith."[17]

"The seed of Abraham" refers to Jews and to Christians in the NT context (Galatians 3:26-29; 6:16). The promise spoken to Abraham would by extension bless all nations of the earth (Genesis 12:3). Jesus became a man from this man's (Abraham) lineage so all the nations of the earth could be blessed by God's promise to him.

He was made like man *"in all things"* (2:17). He was tempted, suffered, and endured. He was made like His brethren so that He could become as a merciful and faithful high priest (4:14, 15). We have a Lord that understands our weaknesses and is sympathetic to our needs. "To die for everyone meant that Jesus had to enter human life and identify Himself with men; suffering is the badge and lot of the race, and a Savior must be a sufferer, if He is to carry out God's saving purpose."[18]

Introduced in this passage is the idea of Jesus serving as our **High Priest**. It is a concept which will serve as a major portion of Hebrews and will develop more as the homily

---

[17] Daniel H. King, Sr., *Hebrews* in the Truth Commentaries (Bowling Green, KY: Guardian of Truth, 2008), 102.

[18] D. Gene West, *A Student's Commentary on the Treatise to the Hebrews* (Delight, AR: Gospel Light, 2009), 86.

continues. As High Priest Christ's role is **"to make propiti-ation for the sins of the people."** *Propitiation* is a word which can be used with reference to atonement, a means of appeasing, a gift to procure atonement, the one who makes atonement, and the place of atonement. Three other times this word is used in the New Testament (Romans 3:25; 1 John 2:2; 1 John 4:10). Each passage gives its own unique contribution to our consideration of Christ as our propitiation.

From Romans 3:21-25, we learn that our propitiation in Christ is a reality because of *His* righteousness. We were un-righteous in sin but have been made righteous by faith in Christ Jesus and His atoning work of redemption. We cannot be made righteous by the deeds of the law. We cannot be made righteous by our own good deeds. Man could not offer a gift worthy enough to procure his forgiveness, so God of-fered the gift or "propitiation" for us. God sent His Son to reconcile us to Him *in* Christ (2 Corinthians 5:18-21). Through Christ's blood, we who were dead in sin can be made alive in Him (Ephesians 2:4-7; Romans 6:3-7, 11).

Our means of appeasing God's wrath (or propitiation) is the blood of Christ. By His blood we are washed from our sins (Revelation 1:5). We are redeemed by His grace (Ephesians 1:7).

1 John 2:1-2 portrays Christ as a propitiation without partiality. He is an advocate for our sins and a possible advocate for the sins of the whole world. God's Son gave Himself as a ransom for all (1 Timothy 2:4-6). Jesus tasted death for every man (Hebrews 2:9). All men are commanded to repent (Acts 17:30). All men *could* be saved by Christ's atonement, but only the obedient *will* be saved.

1 John 4:9-10 is a passage which teaches of Christ's propitiation perfected. Christ is our propitiation because of God's love for us. God sent His Son, not because of our love for Him, but because of His love for us. We must, therefore, respond to His love by loving one another and obeying Him (1 John 5:3).

From these passages we can learn the propitiation of Christ involves our salvation and atonement. His blood is the means of atonement. He was given as the only gift whereby we might procure atonement. His cross is the place of atonement, the Christian's altar (Hebrews 13:10).

"He is able to aid those who are tempted" (2:18). Jesus understands the battles faced by His church in the world. The writer is making clear to his readers that their Savior will not abandon His people when they need Him. We will read later in Hebrews that "He will never leave us or forsake us" (Hebrews 13:5) and that He "ever lives to make intercession" for us (Hebrews 7:25). When facing life's battles, Christians must consider Jesus. The power of Christ is manifested throughout the gospels over nature, demons, sicknesses and diseases, sin, and even death itself. The power of Christ should be manifested in the lives of His people as well (see 1 Corinthians 15:10; 2 Corinthians 13:4-6). Indeed, "If God is for us, who can be against us?" (Romans 8:31)

Summary

With a very logical and skillful use of the scriptures, the writer of Hebrews has reminded his readers of the deity of Jesus, the reason for the humanity of Christ, and the spiritual blessings found only in Him. Only in Jesus can our relationship with God be restored. Only in Christ will we know victory over the devil. Only through His atonement and standing as our High Priest will God forgive our sins.

Leaving His heavenly home, only to return to His throne crowned with glory and honor, Christ Jesus condescended to sinful man, became man, tasted death for everyone, and has offered a great salvation to every man through His gospel. Thy throne, thy scepter, thy kingdom O' God is forever and ever. Amen.

Section Two
Christ Is Greater than Moses and Joshua
3:1 – 4:16

To this point the writer of Hebrews has stated the importance of the verbally inspired word of God in the development of God's relationship with man. God spoke His word first through blessed men of old, but now in this last age He has spoken to us by His own Son.

We have also come to appreciate the credentials of Christ through the inspired writer of Hebrews. Jesus is the brightness of God's glory. He is both Son of God and Son of man. He is greater than the angels. Yet, He became lower than the angels to bring salvation and reconciliation to man. All of which has been said so that we might value the complete and incomparable sufficiency of Christ as Savior of the world. It is Jesus who is distinctively crowned with glory and honor by the Father and He must be so crowned by man as well, if man is to be saved.

"Therefore, holy brethren, partakers of the heavenly calling…" (3:1). Just as the writer stated "therefore," or in

common terms, "because of this," at the beginning of chapter two, he does so here. On this occasion, the writer is connecting the place of Jesus as a "merciful and faithful High Priest" (2:17-18) with the need to "hold fast our confession" (4:14). To connect these points, the writer walks us through the history of Israel in the wilderness and admonishes his readers to "beware" and to "exhort one another" to "hold fast the beginning of our confidence steadfast to the end" (3:12-14).

The writer begins the connection of 2:17 and 4:14 by addressing his readers as **holy brethren** (3:1). "Only here in the New Testament are Christians called holy brethren (*adelphoi hagioi*). The phrase is a combination of two familiar designations of Christians. They are frequently called brethren (cf. Romans 1:13; 1 Corinthians 1:10; 2 Corinthians 1:8) and 'saints' (hagioi; Romans 1:7; 1 Corinthians 1:2; 2 Corinthians 1:1). Holy is the adjective form in English of 'saints.'"[1]

Holiness denotes the idea of being set apart, consecrated, and sanctified. From what were they set apart and to what extent were they set apart? The answer we offer concerning

---

[1] James Thompson, *The Letter to the Hebrews* in The Living Word Commentaries (Austin, TX: R.B. Sweet, 1971), 48.

these early Christian readers, we must also acknowledge to be true for Christian readers today.

Christians have been set apart from the world, or more specifically, Satan's rule in the world. The world lies in wickedness under his sway (1 John 5:19). When a soul is converted, he is taken out of the kingdom of darkness and added to the Lord's kingdom or church (Colossians 1:13). The Christian is set apart, or sanctified, through the washing of water by the word (Ephesians 5:26). When a person is baptized into Christ, he is washed in His blood and receives forgiveness of sin.[2] The sinner is made holy by the grace of God through the atoning blood of Christ.

As followers of Christ, Paul exhorts, "Therefore having these promises, beloved, let us cleanse ourselves from all filthiness of the flesh and spirit, perfecting holiness in the fear of God" (2 Corinthians 7:1).

The newborn saint has a *heavenly calling*. The calling is heavenly because (1) it comes from heaven to man; and (2) it leads man to heaven. It is a "calling" because it is a responsibility or divine purpose incumbent upon the new Christian

---

[2] For further information about baptism in God's plan of salvation, read John 3:3-7; Mark 16:15-16; Acts 2:38; Acts 22:16; Romans 6:3-4; Galatians 3:26-27; Colossians 2:11-13; 1 Peter 3:21.

to keep the mission of Christ alive as the word of truth is preached to every creature. A Christian is not born anew to continue living the same way he has done before. He must put off the old man and be renewed in the spirit of his mind (Ephesians 5:22-23). One is not born again to inactivity but proactivity. His new birth is unto "good works" (Ephesians 2:10). He is now a "partaker" in this heavenly calling. He becomes a laborer together with his brethren and with God (1 Corinthians 3:9). The challenge before every Christian is to walk worthy of this calling or "vocation" in Christ Jesus (Ephesians 4:1). Such essential terms only serve to reinforce the message of the writer to his readers.

The connection between Hebrews 2:17 and 4:14 and the instruction to "hold fast the beginning of our confidence steadfast to the end" (3:12-14) begins with an exhortation to *"consider the Apostle and High Priest of our confession, Christ Jesus"* **(3:1).** Hebrews 3:1 is the only time in the Bible that we find Jesus referred to as an "Apostle." But, when considering that the meaning of the word denotes one who has been sent or commissioned with a message, it is fitting. The writer of Hebrews is continuing to emphasize the fact that our Lord is the Father's messenger sent from heaven (cf. John 12:49; 14:24).

The two-fold ministry of Christ is presented in this text through the use of these terms. Christ came to earth to preach His Father's word. He was the supreme messenger or *Apostle* sent from God. God had one Son, and He made Him a preacher (see Luke 4:18-19, 43; Luke 5:31-32; John 18:37). He is the Apostle of our confession.

To what end and for what purpose did Jesus preach the gospel, but to save man from sin? His preaching would have been incomplete, had He not tasted death for every man and made propitiation for the sins of the people (Hebrews 2:9, 17). By referring to Jesus as our *High Priest*, the writer is recognizing Christ's work in providing atonement for the sins of the people by His precious blood. Christ came to make full atonement for mankind's sin (see Matthew 1:21; Mark 10:45; Luke 19:10). He is a Messenger sent from God and He now serves as High Priest over the house of God. We also remember from Hebrews 1:8 that He is King. Jesus is therefore Prophet (Apostle/Messenger), Priest (High Priest over the House of God), and King (reigning with righteousness over His kingdom, the church).

As we work through this text we are reminded that Jesus came to earth to deal with one issue and one issue alone –

man in sin. He did not come to concern Himself with politics, economics, or the social issues of the day. He came to preach the gospel and to die for sin. Both facets of His divine mission were essential to solving the problem of man's sin. We are "clean by the word" He has spoken (John 15:3) and as we live according to it, we are cleansed daily by His blood (1 John 1:7ff).

If the word will be accepted and followed as a rule for life by all men, the political and social problems we face in the world will also be removed. The world is as it is because it is in rebellion to God. Man's rebellion toward God is the reason for wars and rumors of wars, greed and poverty, corruption and deceit. Only in Christ can the world be saved from itself. Only in Christ will man find peace with God, peace with self, and peace with his neighbor. Only in Christ will man experience life as it is truly meant to be lived. The preaching and propitiation of Christ has qualified Him, and Him alone, to be called the Apostle and High Priest of our confession.

With the great truth of the work and ministry of Christ placed before the readers, they must now consider Christ Jesus *"who was faithful to Him who appointed Him."* When considering Christ, the writer continues to place before the reader the Lord's faithfulness to God (3:2ff.). The faithfulness of Christ should stimulate faithfulness in the life of the believer. Our Lord faced the cross with the determination of "Not My will but Thy will be done." So too must the Christian face every decision in life.

The Father's appointment of the Son is compared to that of Moses (3:2-19). God called Moses from the house of his father-in-law in Midian to return to Egypt to address Pharoah. Moses was appointed by God as a spokesmen and representative of God's blessed will. The writer concludes that Moses was faithful in all His (God's) house (v.2) but that Christ "has been counted worthy of more glory than Moses, inasmuch as He who built the house has more honor than the house" (v.3). Moses was faithful as a *servant* in God's house (v.5). He is to be praised as such. Moses is greatly remembered throughout the scriptures and was even highly honored to be on the Mount of Transfiguration (Matthew 17:3). He was the great lawgiver and a prophet unequaled in his relationship with God (Deuteronomy 34:10). But *"Christ as a Son over His own house"* **(3:6)** cannot be rivaled by any prophet, priest, or king – not even Moses.[3]

---

[3] cf. Hebrews 12:18-29

Christ is the builder of the house (v.3) and has honor not only as the builder but as the Son (v.6). Moses is truly worthy of our esteem and honor. Yet, the point remains, if Moses is worthy of such honor, what about the One of whom he spoke (cf. Deuteronomy 18:15-19; John 5:45-47; Matthew 17:5)?

The house of God is His church (1 Timothy 3:15). His church was built by Christ (Matthew 16:16-19) and purchased with His blood (Acts 20:28). No man can build another, not even the foundation (1 Corinthians 3:11). No man can purchase another. Man is not, nor has he ever been commissioned by God to be a church builder. Once more, Jesus stands alone.

Herein we note that the writer of Hebrews was not concerned with building another house. Rather, he was reminding his brethren of their place in God's house – *"whose house we are, if we hold fast the confidence and the rejoicing of the hope firm to the end"* **(v.6).** The exhortation to remain faithful to God continues from this qualifying condition. "If" qualifies the state of the person subject to the condition of remaining part of the Lord's house. We are His house *if*…. What is the condition? Christians must hold fast the confidence and the rejoicing of the hope firm to the end.[4]

The following verses (3:7-4:16) continue to enlighten and remind the reader of the importance of holding fast to one's faith in God. The writer returns to the wilderness wanderings of Israel and the rebellious attitudes the Israelites manifested toward God. He does this to illustrate to his Christian readers how not to think and act toward God and the consequences which will be brought upon them if they likewise harden their hearts and rebel against His Son.

"Therefore, as the Holy Spirit says…" **(3:7).** Once again, the reader is reminded that God has spoken and the result of His verbal communication with man is the written word (1:1-2; 2:1-4). The writer quotes from David (Psalm 95:7-11) but credits the Holy Spirit as the one speaking. In 4:7, he will use the same passage again and credit David. The writer does so because he is aware that "Holy men of God spoke as they were moved by the Holy Spirit" (2 Peter 1:21). The "Spirit of Christ" was in them and causing them to prophesy of the grace to come (1 Peter 1:10-12).

---

[4] Three early manuscripts do not contain the phrase "firm to the end" but it is found again in 3:14. The instruction stands regardless of the manuscript variants.

"Today if you will hear His voice…" **(3:7-11).** In 3:6, the writer placed a qualifying condition before the reader to consider the importance of holding fast to God. He repeats the use of qualifying conditions in scripture by returning to Psalm 95:7-11. He cites and applies the passage for his readers over the forthcoming verses.

"If you will hear His voice" denotes the ability of man to choose to receive or reject the word of God. If man will hear and receive God's word, he will withstand the temptation to rebel against God and suffer the fury of His anger. If man rejects God's word, rebellion and apostasy will result. God punished those who rebelled against Him in the wilderness[5] and swore *"They shall not enter My rest"* **(v.11).** In verse 18 of this chapter, we learn that these Israelites did not enter the Promised Land because of unbelief.

You will observe that they were not nonbelievers. The Israelites believed in God. "Unbelief" characterized their attitude toward God's word. The Israelites did not believe the word of God applied to them. They did not believe God meant what He said. They did not take His word seriously.

---

[5] Another reference to this comparison can be found in 1 Corinthians 10:1-12.

As a result, not one person in this entire generation of murmuring, rebellious malcontents entered the Promised Land. Not one murmuring, rebellious malcontent will enter heaven either. The writer continues to admonish and exhort his brethren to remain faithful with this is mind.

"Take heed, brethren..." (3:12-13). The possibility of becoming hardened through the "deceitfulness of sin" is possible for any Christian. A person becomes a child of God by faith, penitence, and obedience. One must obey certain conditions or commandments given by God. The word "if" demonstrates that there are conditions and promises predicated upon our choices The NT is full of passages instructing saints and sinners alike using conditional qualifying statements.[6]

The Christian must continue believing, repenting of sin, and obeying the Lord. The terms of the covenant do not end when the covenant is entered. The Lord Himself said, "No one, having put his hand to the plow, and looking back, is fit

---

[6] Take, for instance, 1 Corinthians 15:1-2: "Moreover, brethren, I declare to you the gospel which I preached to you, which also you received and in which you stand, by which also you are saved, *if* you hold fast that word which I preached to you—*unless* you believed in vain." Also consider, "...but Christ as a Son over His own house, whose house we are *if* we hold fast the confidence and the rejoicing of the hope firm to the end" (Hebrews 3:6).

for the kingdom of God" (Luke 9:62). Paul warned the Corinthians, "Therefore let him who thinks he stands take heed lest he fall" (1Corinthians 10:12). The manner of life for a Christian should be characterized by holiness and godliness (2 Peter 3:11). Christians need to be diligent to make their calling and election sure by adding to their faith (2 Peter 1:5-11), that is, by growing in the grace and knowledge of the Lord (2 Peter 3:18) and maturing in Christ (Hebrews 5:11ff.).

It is possible to depart from the living God through the deceitfulness of sin. If this happens, God has provided a way to be *restored* (Galatians 6:1-2) and *converted* (James 5:19-20) to the faith. To *restore* is to put that brother or sister in the order of the former condition, even with all the fullness of Christian fellowship that once existed. The erring Christian must remember, repent, and return. "Remember therefore from where you have fallen; repent and do the first works" (Revelation 2:5).

Paul said, "If a man is *overtaken* in any trespass…" (Galatians 6:1). The sin has taken control or overtaken the man to direct his thoughts, words, or deeds. It is not merely that the brother has sin which he needs to confess to God, for every Christian has such a need. The sin of this man has subdued his spirit and subjugated his soul so as to mar his influence for good and to cause him to wander from the fold of God.

He has allowed sin to have dominion (Genesis 4:7) and reign over his mortal body (Romans 6:12) and inner man (Romans 8:7). This brother should be considered as one who needs to be restored to his former place. His sin has caused him to defect from the truth and divorce himself from Christ. By being overtaken in his sins, he has walked out on the fellowship he had with God and the church, which is in Christ.

God did not leave him. God will never leave us or forsake us (Hebrews 13:5). The wayward child left God. The erring child of God has essentially divorced himself from the most sacred of all his relationships. Through *the deceitfulness of sin*, he has departed from the living God. While the Savior teaches that no man is able "to pluck" us out of the Father's hand (John 10:28-29), even this is conditioned upon our hearing His voice and following Him (John10:27). We have the promise that as long as we are hearing and following Christ we *"shall never perish."* It is when we quit hearing and following Christ that we depart from God.

It is God's will that we walk in His light, not in the darkness of sin (1 John 1:6-10). Faithful Christians are in fellowship with God. Being in fellowship with God requires walking in the light and results in continued fellowship with all others also in fellowship with God. The blessing inherent with such providential fellowship remains: "the blood of Jesus Christ His Son cleanses us from all sin."

One of the essential factors in overcoming the devil and maintaining a steadfast faith in Christ is through the help and encouragement of each other. ***"Exhort one another daily."*** Here we have the antidote for sinful, unbelieving hearts.[7] The verb *parakalein* can mean to exhort (NKJV), to encourage (NIV), but should be considered as "a mixture of both warning and encouragement, designed to motivate those who receive it to persevere in faith, hope, and love."[8]

"For we have become partakers of Christ..." **(3:14-19).** Herein we find once again that the Christian is a partaker with Christ in His ministry to save the world (cf. 3:1). Also repeated is the exhortation to "hear His voice" or "listen to Him." If we will keep listening to what God has said, we will

---

[7] David G. Peterson, *Hebrews: An Introduction and Commentary* in the Tyndale New Testament Commentaries (Downers Grove, IL: IVP, 2020), 114.
[8] Ibid.

(1) hold our confidence until the end; (2) keep our hearts from becoming hardened; and ultimately (3) enter His rest at the end of our pilgrim journey.

We consider Jesus when we *hold fast our faith from beginning to end.* If the children of Israel would have done this, they would not have perished in the wilderness (Numbers 14). If they had done this, they would have entered the Promised Land. If we hold fast, we will enter our Promised Land of heaven. But, if we provoke the Lord through our unbelief, we will ultimately suffer just as those who fell in the wilderness.

The Israelites had the message God spoke through Moses. Yet, they disobeyed through unbelief. Consequently, their hearts were hardened.[9] "An examination of the passage in which the text occurs will show the differing terms that are used to describe the failure of the people; sin, unbelief, disobedience. They are synonymous terms. They heard the word, but proved their practical unbelief by disobedience; and the result was that they lost their sensitiveness to the Divine order."[10] The warning for the readers should be clear:

---

[9] G. Campbell Morgan, *God's Last Word to Man: Studies in Hebrews* (Grand Rapids, MI: Baker Book House, 1974), 50.
[10] Ibid.

Do not let this happen to you! Beware, encourage each other, and hold fast to the end.

"Therefore...let us fear..." (4:1). While "fear" often denotes reverence and respect toward God in scripture, such a definition does not entirely fit the context of the passage. "Genuine fear of facing the wrath of God is a legitimate motive for obedience. The original readers of Hebrews may well have been afraid at the prospect of facing persecution again, but it is more important to fear the anger of God than the hostility of men (Matthew 10:28)."[11] Such godly fear is necessary for obedience and must never be disregarded as a lack of faith (see Ecclesiastes 12:13; 2 Corinthians 5:10, 11; Philippians 2:12; Hebrews 12:28, 29).

We properly consider Jesus by fearing Him, by acknowledging His power and judgment with reverence, respect, and obedience to His word. While taking confidence in the love of God as a Father ultimately casts out fear of judgment for faithful Christians (1 John 4:18), piety should always characterize our thoughts of God. Fear is certainly an appropriate emotion for a Christian when considering the consequences of sinful decisions.

---

[11] McClister, *Hebrews*, 158.

***"For indeed the gospel was preached to us…"* (4:2-10).**
The preaching of the gospel (good news) did not profit the Israelites in the wilderness because they did not receive it with faith. True faith requires more than a mere mental acknowledgement of God. True faith is always joined with obedience to His word (see John 8:30ff.; Romans 10:17; James 2:19ff.).

In verse three we learn that God's ***works were finished*** from the foundation of the world.[12] James offered a similar statement during the Jerusalem conference of Acts 15, affirming, "Known to God from eternity are all His works" (15:18). God's finished works are found in the natural realm as well as the spiritual. The universe was spoken into existence, finished, and set in order at their creation. So too were God's plans in the spiritual order.

God knew man would sin. He planned to send His Son as a sin offering. He planned for His Son to give hope to all nations through the gospel. He determined that man must be obedient to this gospel. God determined from the foundation of the world that the gospel would be preached to Jews and

---

[12] Consider also: Matthew 25:34; John 17:24; Acts 17:30; Ephesians 2:1-11; Revelation 13:8.

Gentiles alike, thus creating one new nation, a royal priest-hood, a spiritual house built upon the one and only founda-tion of Jesus Christ. We read of this prophecy in Daniel 2:44 and we read that it has now been received in Hebrews 12:28. The church is that kingdom that shall stand forever. Every-thing we do according to the scriptures is done according to the eternal purpose and foreknowledge of God.

God exercised His foreknowledge while maintaining His freedom to interact with man according to man's responses to Him. God's foreknowledge did not prevent Him from an-swering prayer, sparing the innocent, testing His people, or punishing the wicked. As man came to understand the right-eousness of God, and that he should respond obediently to Him, the foundation for a relationship based upon interaction and responsiveness between Creator and creature was clearly solidified.

Proper consideration of Christ also includes proper con-sideration of *His rest*. For us, His rest is heaven. Jesus has prepared a place for us (John 14:1-3). Heavenly rest can only come through Christ (John 14:6). It is not in Moses, Joshua, or David. The "rest" the writer is speaking of re-mains eternally for the people of God because of our faithful Apostle and High Priest. When we enter this rest, we can cease from our labors (Revelation 14:13). Our faith will become sight. Heaven will be our home.

***"Let us therefore be diligent to enter that rest..."* (4:11-13).** In this life, we must be diligent to enter the heavenly rest.[13] Diligence is required to make one's "calling and election sure." The same steadfast measure of diligence must be given until the end (Hebrews 6:10). No one is going to heaven by accident, by backing into it, or by proxy. God rewards those who diligently seek Him (Hebrews 11:6). Diligent intention and purpose of heart to love God and follow His blessed will is commanded of all men and must characterize anyone and anything called "Christian."

Obviously, that which is required of man is not beyond the reach of man, but it does require effort. God is not requiring more than man is able to do, but He is requiring of man, nonetheless. In a day when many wish to view the Christian religion as being a nearly effortless religion, scriptures like this call us back to the true nature of the faith. It seems to us to be rather insulting to God to think that He would have allowed His Son to suffer and die only to give man a religion which expects nothing, requires nothing, and

---

[13] Please read Matthew 5:16ff.; 1 Corinthians 15:58; Ephesians 2:10; Titus 2:11-15; Revelation 20:12-13.

accomplishes nothing as far as true reformation of will and renewal of mind is concerned.

Did Christ die so that man could continue to conduct the same wretched manner of life which made him an enemy to God in the first place (Isaiah 59:1, 2; James 4:4; 1 Peter 3:12)? "God forbid! How shall we who are dead to sin live any longer therein?" Should not the cross evoke in man a desire to be like Christ as nearly as is humanly possible? Does His death not bring to bear on the human conscience the seriousness of sin and the sad state of rebellion which exists between the human race and its Creator? If man can enter the rest of heaven while living in rebellion to God, was He then unjust in forbidding the Israelites entrance into the Promised Land for sins less severe?

Incumbent upon every man is the necessity to give a diligent and honest examination of the Christian religion from the Christian scriptures. What has the Lord and His holy apostles to say about "the faith once delivered"? Let us do as Saul of Tarsus and ask, "Lord, what will you have me to do?" But to diminish the Christian faith into a do nothing, be nothing religion is insulting to the Spirit of grace, contrary to the word of God, and meaningless to the salvation of the soul.

If we are not faithfully working the works of Christ, for which we are born again to work, we will fall after "the same example of disobedience" the Israelites fell in the wilderness. Coupled with the exhortation to faithfulness is a reminder of the living and active power of God's word. ***"The word of God is living and active" (4:12).*** Obedience and disobedience to God are determined by His word. The word of God is living (cf. 1 Peter 1:23). Heaven and earth will pass away, but the word of the Lord will abide forever (Matthew 24:35). God's word remains and will remain as the standard of judgment (cf. John 12:48).

While God's works are finished, and His mind is settled, His word remains active in discerning the thoughts and the intents of our hearts. "The Lord searches all hearts and understands all the intent of the thoughts" (1 Chronicles 28:9).

As a sword, the word of God has two edges or two sides and both are equally sharp. The Bible contains words of warning and comfort; words of rebuke and commendation; words of judgment and promise. Both aspects of the word of God must be taught, understood, and respected. Consider the Psalmist's respectful consideration of all aspects of the word of God:

"The law of the Lord is perfect, refreshing the soul. The statutes of the Lord are trustworthy, making wise the simple. The precepts of the Lord are right, giving joy to the heart. The commands of the Lord are radiant, giving light to the eyes. The fear of the Lord is pure, enduring forever. The decrees of the Lord are firm, and all of them are righteous. They are more precious than gold, than much pure gold; they are sweeter than honey, than honey from the honeycomb. By them your servant is warned; in keeping them there is great reward. But who can discern their own errors? Forgive my hidden faults. Keep your servant also from willful sins; may they not rule over me. Then I will be blameless, innocent of great transgression. May these words of my mouth and this meditation of my heart be pleasing in your sight, Lord, my Rock and my Redeemer" (Psalm 19:7-14).

The word is the "sword of the Spirit" (Ephesians 6:17). It is the one offensive piece in the battle armament of the Christian soldier. The Christian can use it to defend himself from the sword swipes of the enemy and it can be used to penetrate the heart of every false thing.

The writer also asserts that *"no creature is hidden from His sight"* **(4:13).** Man can hide a great many things from others, and possibly even from himself, but man cannot hide anything from God (Genesis 3). Man is completely vulnerable and exposed before God. Helpless.[14]

---

[14] King, *Hebrews*, 140.

However, once a person comes to consider Jesus as a merciful and faithful High Priest, one will realize the foolishness of even attempting to hide sin from God. Our Lord knows our sins and desires to help us overcome them. We are completely safe in our vulnerability and helplessness before God because He truly loves us and longs to save us. He is not our enemy – far from it! He is our Father. And our Lord Jesus is the best Friend we will ever know.

"Seeing then that we have a great High Priest..." **(4:14-16).** The priesthood of Christ will become the primary focus for the writer for the next few chapters. The concluding verses of chapter 4 serve as a transition from this section of the Hebrew homily to the next section which will focus primarily upon Christ's priesthood. The pivot occurs by looking back at the statements concerning Christ as High Priest (2:17; 3:1) and looking ahead at the characteristics of His priesthood. Christ has passed into the heavens and is interceding for us at the right hand of the Father. He does not intercede from earth but from heaven. He intercedes because He is sensitive to our weaknesses and trials. The Lord was *in all points* tempted as we are. He knows the battle we fight daily against "all that is in the world, the lust of the flesh, and the lust of the eyes, and the pride of life" (1 John 2:16).

Seeing that Jesus knows and that Jesus cares, "let us" (1) hold fast our confession (v.14) and "come boldly (with confidence) to the throne of grace..." (4:16). Some English versions offer the rendering, "let us draw near." The phrase is used seven times in Hebrews. Concerning this expression, Lightfoot notes, "Since in the Old Testament it is used of priests and their approach to God (Lev. 21:17-21, etc.), the author's use and application of the term suggest that the priestly privilege of access to God is now extended to all Christians."[15]

As we draw near to God, let us remember that our High Priest is both merciful and faithful (2:17), granting mercy *and* help in our time of need. Grace, mercy, and help – these three words command the attention of the reader and describe perfectly what may be found in Christ as High Priest.

Through Christ, we are not only granted mercy (forgiveness), but also help in our time of need. It is a sad tragedy indeed to know that souls suffer simply because they do not seek the help of the Savior. The suffering Christian is not coming to a throne of judgment, but to a throne of grace.

---

[15] Neil R. Lightfoot, *Jesus Christ Today: A Commentary on the Book of Hebrews* (Abilene, TX: Bible Guides, 2001), 104.

God, who knows all things (1 John 3:20), knows the sin, the suffering, and the solution. Christ desires to help. The Father desires to show mercy. Yet, the afflicted soul often remains stubborn and toils to solve life's problems without God. It cannot be done and should not be attempted. Consider that it is a "throne of grace" and the one who sits upon it is One who suffers with His people through their trials and temptations. He knows and cares and "He ever lives to make intercession for us" (7:25).

We cannot hide our needs from God. As previously affirmed, no creature is hidden from His sight. Christ is faithful and merciful. Man must trust that He is. When the troubles and temptations of life press us to the earth, let us call out to God from there. In our time of need, let us come with confidence to the throne of grace and find mercy and help in time of need.

Summary

As the second section of Hebrews concludes, the third section begins. In the first two chapters we were brought to a consideration of Jesus' greatness in comparison to any prophet and every angel. None like Jesus has ever or will ever grace our presence again on this earth. In the last two chapters, the readers have be made keenly aware of the faults and failures of the children of Israel who disobeyed God through His servant Moses. We are warned not to allow sin to harden our hearts into a state of unfaithfulness and fall because of unbelief.

The promised rest for the people of God remains in heaven, but we must be diligent to enter that rest. We must hold fast to our confession of Jesus as the Christ, the Son of the living God. God's children must always come with confidence to the throne of His grace in our times of need. Christians cannot and must not attempt to fight their battle against the devil without the grace, mercy, and help of God.

Section Three

The Nature and Scope of Christ's High Priesthood
5:1 – 7:28

Being Hebrews themselves, the first readers would have been familiar with the qualifications for priesthood, particularly the high priesthood. Hebrews 5:1-10 presents a summary of the qualifications for a high priest. He had to come from among men – i.e., he had to be human; and he had to receive his authority from God. The forthcoming verses serve as confirmation of 4:14-16 by showing what true priesthood requires and how Christ fulfills these requirements.[1]

As he did with the prophets and angels in chapters one and two, the writer compares Christ as our High Priest and the Aaronic high priesthood according to the law. Every comparison offers an affirmative argument to amplify the supremacy of Christ over the religious system He embodied and fulfilled. The writer does so while also offering a heart-felt appeal for obedience and steadfastness to Him. To be

---

[1] W.H. Griffith Thomas, *Hebrews: A Devotional Commentary* (Grand Rapids, MI: Eerdmans, 1970), 62.

sure, the high priest of the Aaronic order was greatly esteemed among first century Jews. Coffman reminds us of the measure of respect rendered to the high priest at that time.

> "Without doubt, the earthly splendor of the Jewish high priest was a factor of seductive influence on Christians, especially those of Jewish background. His rich robes, the extravagantly ornate breastplate, the unique privilege of entering the Holy of Holies on the day of atonement, his status as judge and president of the Sanhedrin, his dramatic influence as the official representative of the Jewish nation, more especially at a time when they had no king, the traditional descent of the office from the sons of Aaron and reaching all the way back to the Exodus, and the grudging respect paid to the office, even by Roman conquerors – all these things and many others elevated the Jewish high priest to a position of isolated splendor in the eyes of the people."[2]

As we read through the forthcoming passages and consider the meaning of the text itself, we will do well to keep in mind the great honor and esteem associated with the office of high priest. The comparison and excellence of Christ as High Priest is no small point to consider.

"Every high priest is appointed from among men to represent them in matters relating to God..." (5:1-4). Hebrews

---

[2] Coffman, *Hebrews*, 97-98.

5:1a presents the essential definition of a priest.[3] He is appointed from among men, and he is a representative of man in matters relating to God. The verse continues with a clear statement of the function of the high priest in that he is "to offer gifts and sacrifices for sins." According to the law, any sacrifice offered daily was to be done at the door of the tabernacle of the congregation by the priests (Leviticus 1-7). Any sacrifice offered on the Day of Atonement was to be offered within the veil of the tabernacle by the high priest. The high priest was an intercessor, standing between man and God, offering both gifts and sacrifices for sins.

Another essential characteristic for a priest was that he was *"able to deal gently with those who are ignorant and misguided, since he himself is beset by weakness"* (5:2). What good is a minister of the people if he is not sympathetic? While the OT prophet denounced the sins of the people and called for repentance or else destruction, the priest was to be sympathetic, and to aid in the forgiving of sins.[4] The idea of dealing "gently" means to "have compassion." "The priest had to decide whether a sacrifice for sin could be given legally (Lev. 10-11; Deut. 12:8-13; 24:8; 33:10; Mal.

---

[3] Ibid.

[4] Don Earl Boatman, *Helps from Hebrews* in the Bible Study Textbook Series (Joplin, MO: College Press, 1960), 148.

97

2:7)."[5] If a man sinned through ignorance or in error, or in an occasion where temptation might obscure for a time the guilt, a sacrifice could be given, sin be forgiven (Numbers 15:22-29). If it was the sin of the high hand, in the spirit of haughty insolence, there could be no sacrifice. The transgressor could be put to death at the testimony of two or three witnesses (Numbers 15:30.31; Deuteronomy 17:6). The high priest dealing gently could sometimes bring a person to repentance.[6]

Being also beset by weaknesses, the priest "is obligated to offer sacrifices for his own sins, as well as for the sins of the people" (5:3). No matter how upright a priest might have been, none were sinlessly perfect. Atonement had to be made for their sins before they were fit to offer sacrifices for the sins of others.

"No one takes this honor upon himself; he must be called by God, just as Aaron was" **(5:4).** The role of high priest was granted by God and those who served in this capacity were recognized as having been divinely called to it. "No man can of his own accord set himself up as high priest, nor can he hold the office validly by the gift of an earthly

---

[5] Ibid.
[6] Ibid.

authority."[7] Those claiming to be priests today in the Roman Church and others without the authority of scripture would do well to consider this passage.

"High priest" was not merely a titled to be claimed or purchased. Nor was it an office to be granted by election. Both the honor and the authority of the high priest were granted by God. "He is an intruder who is not called of God, as was Aaron."[8] Aaron was ordained as high priest by divine appointment (Exodus 28:1ff.; Leviticus 8:1ff.; Numbers 16:5; 17:5; 18:1ff.; Psalm 105:26). Others who made offerings in time of emergency exercised their intercession and offered sacrifices by a direct and special call from God (cf. 1 Samuel 6:3ff.).[9]

***"So also Christ did not take upon Himself the glory of becoming a high priest…"* (5:5-6).** Just as Aaron received his calling, honor, and glory from God as high priest, *"So also"* did Jesus. It is by the will of the Father that the Son is glorified as High Priest over the house of God which is His church. "If our author is to sustain his thesis that Jesus is His

[7] F.F. Bruce, *The Epistle to the Hebrews*, 92.
[8] Matthew Henry, *Matthew Henry's Commentary on the Whole Bible* (vol. 6): *Acts to Revelation* (Peabody, MA: Hendrickson Publishers, 1991), 732.
[9] Bruce, 93.

people's great high priest, he must produce comparable evidence of a divine call in His case."[10]

Our Lord's priesthood, however, does not follow the course of Aaron and the Old Law. Because Jesus was not a Levite, some Hebrews might have chosen not to consider Jesus as their high priest. He was born of the tribe of Judah. Rather, just as Melchizedek was a priest who interceded for Abraham (cf. Genesis 14:13ff.), Christ is our intercessor (Romans 8:34); and it is by Christ that we have our sacrifice for sin (Ephesians 5:2) and can become a living sacrifice ourselves (Romans 12:1ff.). In fact, it is by the sacrifice of Christ that even the high priests under the first covenant will be saved (Romans 3:25; Hebrews 9:15). He is the embodiment and fulfillment of the High Priesthood. Every priest from Melchizedek down through the stream of time only anticipated and foreshadowed the Priesthood of Christ.

Consider the arguments used by the writer of Hebrews from the OT scriptures as he recognized Christ as High Priest. First, He must be considered thus because He is God's Son (Psalm 2:7). Secondly, He is a priest "forever" after the order of Melchizedek (Psalms 110:4). He has received His

---

[10] Ibid.

role as High Priest from God, not the law or Aaronic lineage. As such, He will serve in this capacity "forever" – until the end of the world.

Melchizedek provides a precedent proving that not every high priest had to be a Levite to offer sacrifices pleasing to God. The priesthood depended upon the dispensation in which one lived and the law which one was under. We are now in a different dispensation and under a different law. Therefore, a change of the priesthood was coupled with the change of the law (Hebrews 7:12).

"During the days of Jesus' earthly life, He offered up prayers and petitions…" ***(5:7).*** The Hebrew writer takes us back to the Garden of Gethsemane. He cried out and was heard, yet He still had to endure the cross. Just because the Father's answer was "no" did not mean that Jesus' prayer went unheard. Nor did it mean that God did not love Him. Too many times Christians lose heart and doubt their relationship with God if a prayer is not answered affirmatively. Jesus cried out with tears, enduring sorrow and suffering as He dreaded the prospect of the cross. Yet even though He dreaded the cross and sweat drops of blood in His grief, He obediently endured, and became the author (or the source) of our eternal salvation.

"Although He was a Son, He learned obedience from what He suffered" **(5:8).** Jesus learned the consequence of living obediently to the Father. Coffman explains, "His perfect obedience was the cause of bitter hatred against him and provided the occasion for every blow that fell upon his person. That hatred of Christ was exactly in the pattern of the hatred of Abel, who was murdered by his brother Cain; 'And wherefore slew he him? because his works were evil, and his brother's righteous' (1 John 3:12)."[11]

"And having been made perfect, He became the source of eternal salvation to all who obey Him" **(5:9).** To whom is this salvation granted? Allow the Bible to answer: "to all who obey Him." The sinner must come to God by way of the cross. He cannot come in pride, contempt, or unbelief to God. He must humble himself to God, obey His word, and keep His commandments.

Forgiveness is an executive act. One cannot be forgiven of a debt unless the one with the authority to forgive the debt forgives the debt. God is the only one with the authority to forgive the sin-debt which man owes. One cannot be forgiven and thus reconciled to God without faith, repentance,

---

[11] Coffman, 104.

and obedience. These are the requirements stipulated by God. God has required faith, repentance, and obedience from man beginning with the fall in Eden. The obedience God requires now is to His Son through His gospel (cf. Matthew 7:21-23; 2 Thessalonians 1:7-9; Matthew 28:18-20).

God has determined and set the standard for man's life according to His just nature and commands all men everywhere to obey Him (Acts 17:30-31). Consequently, when man obeys God, he is accepting the gift of God's grace – i.e., the atonement provided by His only-begotten Son, the source of our salvation. If man refuses to obey God, he is rejecting the gift of God's grace; he is rejecting Christ; he is rejecting eternal salvation. The gospel must be preached, believed, and obeyed for a person to be saved (Mark 16:15-16).

Thus, Christ was "designated by God as high priest in the order of Melchizedek" (5:10). He was born as a man to fulfill the requirement of a priest being appointed from among men. Not being a Levite, His priesthood is according to the order of Melchizedek. Jesus has been selected by God, thus fulfilling the requirement to be divinely chosen to the office of High Priest. Being sympathetic to our weaknesses and willing to deal gently with us, He is a faithful and merciful

High Priest. He offers atonement according to His just mercy to all who obey Him.

Greater still, and more excellent than all others, He is the sinlessly perfect Son of God who suffered for His obedience to the Father so that we might live forever in the light of His love. But, when Christians fail to consider Christ and thank God for Him every day, inevitably they will grow dull of hearing. The writer, therefore, voices his displeasure and frustration in the fact that *"we have much to say, and hard to explain, since you have become dull of hearing"* **(5:11).**

Many examples are to be found in the scriptures for this malady of spiritual deafness. One might even call it "selective hearing." Such was the condition of Israel during the time of Isaiah and the prophets (Isaiah 6:9-10) as well as during the time of Paul (Acts 28:25-27). Paul also warned Timothy about those who would have "itching ears" during his ministry and that they would be turning aside from the truth and unto fables (2 Timothy 4:3-4).

It is not merely his own personal displeasure the writer is expressing, but he is voicing the Lord's disappointment in these brethren for their lack of spiritual maturity and loss of enthusiasm for His word. The result of "dull hearing" is a cessation of spiritual growth and thus numerical growth in the body of Christ.

One cannot grow spiritually without the word of God. The church cannot grow numerically without first growing spiritually. A church that does not feast from the word regularly can never grow spiritually. The writer of Hebrews recognized a congregation that did not grow in their knowledge of the word as they should have and thus their spiritual growth was stunted. Interestingly, not one word concerning the church's ongoing numerical growth is mentioned in Hebrews.

"For though by this time…" **(5:12).** The Hebrew brethren needed to be taught again, not because they had been taught incorrectly previously, but because they were spiritually immature and did not continue in the teachings they had received. The brethren had failed to take advantage of the opportunity to learn. It proved impossible for these brethren to grow numerically as they had become numb and dull to the truth. Seeing that they had no interest in learning, how could they have had any interest in teaching others? If a person is not excited to learn, how can he be excited to teach?

Teaching was clearly something expected of them as *"by this time you ought to be teachers."* Teaching is something a Christian *ought* to be doing. Not all teaching is to be done in a public manner. In fact, one might argue that most teaching should be conducted "house to house" or privately as we go throughout life and encounter others along the way. Readiness to answer and defend the faith (1 Peter 3:15) is incumbent upon every Christian of reasonable spiritual maturity. In the estimation of the writer, his readers had been Christians long enough that "by this time" they should have been more advanced in their knowledge of the word and in their ability to teach others.

In Luke 8:5-15 we read the parable of the Sower and the Soils, in which Jesus gave two reasons for a person becoming dull of hearing – (1) trials and temptations and (2) the cares and riches of this life. Ultimately any reason for becoming dull of hearing could fit these two categories. From the context of Hebrews, it appears trials and sufferings may have been the cause of their dullness of hearing. Whatever the reason, it was inexcusable. The writer was calling for his brethren to grow spiritually in Christ and to become skillful in their communication of the word.

"For everyone who partakes only of milk is unskilled in the word of righteousness, for he is a babe" **(5:13).** The metaphor of the milk of the word is also used by Peter (1 Peter 2:2). Milk is the food of "newborn babes," i.e., new converts to Christ. The first principles of the word are to be desired and we are to grow thereby. But, we are not to stay on the first principles. Christians are not to remain babes. God's children must grow from milk to eating meat. *"But solid food belongs to those who are of full age…"* **(5:14).**

As a child grows physically, he advances in his diet from only drinking milk to eventually eating meat. So it is with a Christian. Every Christian should strive to grow in the grace and knowledge of the Lord (2 Peter 3:18). Time, effort, and discipline is required of every individual seeking to grow in knowledge of the word of God. Yet, these brethren were still in need of the first principles. They were still eating milk when they were eating at all. So limited in knowledge were they that they needed to be taught these things again. The recipients needed to learn how to discern good from evil and only by reason of use could their senses be exercised to discern both good and evil.

The Bible has much to say about the characteristic of discernment. Discernment is needed to "destroy arguments and every lofty opinion raised against the knowledge of God, and take every thought captive to obey Christ" (2 Corinthians 10:5, ESV). Discernment is needed to "teach my people the difference between the holy and the common, and show them how to distinguish between the unclean and the clean" (Ezekiel 44:23, ESV). And discernment is needed to "test the spirits to see whether they are from God, for many false prophets have gone out into the world" (1 John 4:1, ESV). Discernment is also of immeasurable value when judging how to deal with one's fellowman. Such was the root of Solomon's prayer, "Give your servant therefore an understanding mind to govern your people, that I may discern between good and evil, for who is able to govern this your great people?" (1 Kings 3:9, ESV).

***"Therefore, leaving the discussion of the elementary principles of Christ, let us go on to perfection…"* (6:1-3)** Just as any minister worth his salt would desire, the writer here offers his help to aid his brethren in their ascent toward perfection, i.e., spiritual maturity. Such is achieved not by abandoning the elementary principles of Christ, but rather the advancement begins with these principles in mind and is established upon them as "the foundation" for learning. Mature Christians do not forget or forsake the lessons learned when they were new to the faith; they add to them. Knowing and cherishing the elementary principles enables a person to grasp the deeper things of God as they are able.

Instead of going into a lengthy discourse of the first principles, the author simply mentions a few examples. Ironically, the principles considered by the writer to be elementary have become some of the most hotly contested doctrines today. *"Repentance from dead works and of faith toward God"* is at the heart of the Christian gospel. What is a Christian if he is not changed and converted as "such were some of you" (1 Corinthians 6:9-11)? Repentance was the answer given during the first gospel sermon (Acts 2:38), it remains the Christian answer to the world's woes today. The world is as it is because it is in a state of rebellion to God. The message of repentance is one of turning from sin and returning to God to be converted (Acts 3:19). Repentance is the transforming of a hardened heart of rebellion into the clean heart created after God in true righteousness. The weakened anemic state of many pulpits is largely due to missing or neglecting a call for repentance.

The doctrine of baptisms in the plural probably refers to John's baptism and the baptism of the Great Commission.

Confusion existed for some concerning the difference between these baptisms. However, such confusion was cleared by those who understood and were grounded in truth regarding the subject (see Apollos in Ephesus, Acts 18-19).

One cannot fully receive or accept the word of God until he has obeyed its teaching by repenting of sin and being baptized. We find that 3,000 souls repented and "gladly received" the word on Pentecost "and were baptized" (Acts 2:38-41). We learn that certain citizens of the city of Samaria "received the word of God" (Acts 8:14) when they accepted the "preaching of the kingdom" and "were baptized" (Acts 8:12). Cornelius and his near friends and kinsmen "received the word of God" when they yielded in obedience to its teaching and were baptized (Acts 10:48).

At baptism, we become united with Christ and are brought into harmony and spiritual union with His death, burial, and resurrection (Romans 6:3-7). According to Paul, baptism stands between the sinner and being freed from his sins. By being baptized into His death, disciples have the promise of being in the likeness of His resurrection, destroying the old man of sin, and thus being freed from the bondage of sin. God has selected the action of baptism to signify the point in which souls are united with the death, burial, and resurrection of Christ. One cannot obey the gospel of the death, burial, and resurrection of Christ without being baptized. One cannot be resurrected unto a new man without a death and burial of the old man.

From Colossians 2:11-13 we can observe that baptism stands between man and (1) putting off the body of the sins of the flesh; (2) being buried with Christ; (3) being raised with Christ through faith in the operation of God; (4) being made alive together with Him; and (5) being forgiven of all trespasses. You will note that Paul has said essentially the same thing and made the same key points pertaining to baptism in this passage as in Romans 6:3-7. Also, let it be observed that the forgiveness found in baptism is not a work of men, but "the working of God" as was clearly stated by the apostle.

Laying on of hands was critical to the first century church. Miraculous gifts were bestowed by the laying on of hands (Acts 8:17; Romans 1:11; 2 Timothy 1:6). Approval and blessings were also conveyed through ceremonies involving the laying on of hands (Acts 6:6; 13:3; 1 Timothy 5:22). Moreover, healing occurred through the laying on of hands (Acts 28:8) accompanied by prayer (James 5:14).

Through the outpouring of the Holy Spirit on the apostles, they were enabled to bestow miraculous gifts to others and confirm the word they were preaching (Hebrews 2:1-4; Mark 16:17-20). When divine revelation ceased, so too did divine confirmation cease (1 Corinthians 13:8, 10).

The resurrection of the dead is also considered an elementary principle. According to John 5:28-29, "all who are in the tombs" will be resurrected at the Lord's return. Not only will the resurrection include the righteous, but also the wicked. Throughout the ages, many have sought to deny the resurrection completely. The Sadducees did so (Mark 12:18-27), as well as a group in Corinth which went as far as to deny the resurrection of Christ (1 Corinthians 15:12). We also learn of such men as Hymenaeus and Philetus who overthrew the faith of some by teaching that the resurrection has already passed (2 Timothy 2:16-18).

Eternal judgment will occur after the heaven and earth have fled away (see Hebrews 1:11-12). Judgment will be rendered according to the word of God and according to our works. Eternity will follow the final judgment.

The doctrine of universal salvation for all mankind (universalism) ignores the plain teachings of scripture pertaining to hell. Any doctrine which is purported to be biblical but ignores the biblical text must itself be ignored by those who cherish the Bible.

Annihilationism is another attempt to disregard the first principle of eternal judgment. The doctrine teaches that the wicked will cease to exist either at the point of death or eventually for their eternal punishment. The Bible teaches that hell is the final place for those who were disobedient to God's word. Those who deny the concept of eternal conscious punishment deny the clear teaching of Jesus Christ.

The most common word used to refer to the length of the punishment for sinners is *aionios*, the adjective form of *aion*. It is used about 67 times to refer to what is endless. When all the passages referring to hell are considered, they clearly indicate that "not extinction in opposition to existence, but torturous existence in the society of evil in opposition to life in the society of God."[12]

The very nature of God demands that the wicked be punished. Punishment is described as something that is terrible,

---

[12] G. R. Beasley-Murray, *The Book of Revelation,* The New Century Bible Commentary, rev. ed. (Grand Rapids, MI: Eerdmans, 1978), 304.

conscious, and never-ending. God provides both the description and the warning as motivation for obedience (Acts 17:30, 31; Romans 2:4-11).

The writer offers no hint of presumption as he vows to move beyond first principles *"if God permits."* We are all in the hands of God and subject to his providential will and sovereignty. "If the Lord wills, we shall live and do this or that" (James 4:15).

"For it is impossible for those who were once enlightened… to renew them again unto repentance" **(6:4-8).** Hebrews 6:4-6 is one of the more difficult passages to interpret in the book. The NT teaches quite often the possibility of restoring a wayward brother (Galatians 6:1-2). We affirm that scripture does not contradict, therefore, we must seek to harmonize the impossibility of renewal spoken here with the possibility of restoration taught in Galatians and other passages. Perhaps our answer can be found in a study of the tenses being used in this text.

Observe, "It is impossible for those who **have once been enlightened** (past tense), who **have tasted the heavenly gift** (past tense), who **have shared in the Holy Spirit** (past tense), who **have tasted the goodness of the word of God** and the powers of the coming age (past tense)—and **then have fallen away** (past tense)—**to be restored** (future tense) to repentance, because they themselves **are crucifying** (present tense) the Son of God all over again and **subjecting** (present tense) Him to open shame" (6:4-6).[13]

Consider who is under consideration. The brother has "been enlightened," that is, he has come to the light of understanding the plan and purpose of God through Christ. He has "tasted of the heavenly gift," possibly referring to salvation but perhaps to a spiritual gift (cf. 1 Corinthians 12:1-11). The brother has "shared in the Holy Spirit," again possibly a spiritual gift has been bestowed, but this could also refer to the indwelling of the Spirit experienced by all Christians (cf. Romans 8:9ff.). The wayward saint has also "tasted the goodness of the word of God and the powers of the coming age," again it is difficult to determine with certainty, but this could refer to a miraculous ability granted, or simply to the glory that shall be revealed in us in heaven (Romans 8:18).

---

[13] The translation cited is from the Berean Study Bible which provides an excellent rendering of the tenses being used. Similar renderings can be found in more widely used English translations like the ESV and NIV.

Having considered the subject of the text, let us observe what he is presently doing and his present condition. He is "crucifying the Son of God all over again" and "subjecting Him to open shame." A serious matter indeed! The brother is in a present and continuing state of rebellion. His rebellion has not only become a shame to himself, but to the church, and more importantly to the Lord. As long as his life is one of willful sin, he is daily crucifying afresh of the Son of God, and there remains no more sacrifice for his sins (Hebrews 10:26). The writer later depicts the rebellious brother's disregard for Christ as trampling Jesus beneath his feet, despising the blood of the covenant as a common thing, and insulting the Spirit of grace (Hebrews 10:29). If he remains in this condition, spiritual renewal will be impossible. His sin will become a "sin unto death" (1 John 5:16).

For restoration to occur, the wayward brother must be converted from the error of his way (James 5:19-20). The erring brother must repent of his sins and confess them to God. Only if he repents, can he be restored. If and when he does repent, the church must reaffirm their love for him (2 Corinthians 2:8). Just as the church cannot extend fellowship to someone not in fellowship with God, the church cannot withhold fellowship to someone in fellowship with God.

116

When the wayward brother makes things right with God, he makes things right with the church.

The question must now be raised as to how he came into this spiritual condition. We return to the warnings previously found in Hebrews to find our answer. If we fail to give an earnest heed to the things of Christ (2:1ff), become hardened by the deceitfulness of sin (3:12-13), and find ourselves dull of hearing (5:11), such apostasy is inevitable. How do we prevent developing such a wretched spiritual condition? Be diligent to enter His rest (4:11), come with confidence to the throne of grace to find mercy and grace to help in time of need (4:16), and progress to perfection and spiritual maturity through growth in the knowledge of His word (6:1).

Herein, we can begin to see why the writer has said these things. He wants his readers to get back to growing in their faith, lest they become hardened in their hearts beyond a point of no return. A person can become so dull of hearing that they simply stop/refuse listening. If they are of this mindset, it is impossible to renew (or reconcile) them with God.

If a Christians falls away, he must do like the prodigal son who came to himself, returned to his father, and confessed his sins. While the prodigal son fell away, he did not fall to the point that he became completely dull to his father's teachings. In this context, it seems that the writer is speaking of the one who falls away and is completely numb to anything pertaining to godliness. Here is a person who is not going to repent, regardless of who they hurt in the process.

Even after having known the power of God perhaps in a miraculous way, some were evidently at risk of becoming beyond reach. They are likened to a field full of thorns and briars, *whose end is to be burned* (v.8). No longer are they producing useful fruit from the blessings received from God (v.7). Instead, they have become a spiritually neglected field, full of the briars of sin, and have returned to the former nature to live once more as children of wrath and dead in sin (cf. Ephesians 2:1-3), which existed before the cultivating hand of grace tended to their condition.

"But, beloved, we are confident of better things concerning you…" **(6:9-12).** While the writer has been doing some stern admonishing, he transitions to offer some vital words of encouragement. He first reminds them of his love for them by referring to them as "beloved" and affirms his confidence in them *"of better things concerning you, and things that accompany salvation."* The writer of Hebrews

provides an example for all ministers of the gospel to have faith in their flock to do and to be right by God. He was basing his confidence on the record of "your work and labor of love which you have shown toward His name, in that you have ministered to the saints, and do minister" (6:10).

God is not unjust to forget these things. God's faithfulness to His children must be noted. He does not want his children to fail. He remembers their good work and loves them for it. Such good works are the fruit of one's faith and salvation. Certainly, these people knew what a living and active faith was like, which provides even more reason for the high expectations placed upon them from the writer. They had done well before; they can do well again.

The "desire" of the writer is expressly stated for *"each one of you to show the same diligence to the full assurance of hope until the end, that you do not become sluggish, but imitate those who through faith and patience inherit the promises"* (6:11-12). Upon reminding them of what they had done and were doing, the writer encourages them not to be sluggish, slothful, or lazy. The idea of being slothful is very closely related to the idea of being dull of hearing. When one becomes dull of learning and then slothful in applying the word, the danger of outright apostasy is increasingly near. Such behavior is usually indicative of slow digression from the truth. Such a person may not even realize their condition until completely overcome by apathy.

Included in his encouragement is a hinting at the great figures from Israel's past as a means of stimulating good works by imitating "those who through faith and patience inherit the promises." Let us paraphrase the thought in this way: "Remember the faith of those who have gone before, and how they inherited the promises because they refused to backslide. Now, be like them." However, these promises can only be received *after* patiently enduring. Abraham is offered as a prime example of a faithful man.

"For when God made a promise to Abraham..." (6:13-15). The Hebrew writer is referring to God's promise to Abraham in Genesis 12:1-3 (see also Isaiah 45:23). He was called at age 75 and promised his posterity would be great (Genesis 12:4). Only after twenty-four years did he learn how God would keep His promise (Genesis 17:1ff.). At the age of 100 Isaac was born to him (Genesis 21:1ff.). "In Isaac's birth Abraham began to see the fulfillment of the promise; and later, with Abraham still believing the promise,

this son was restored to him from death."[14] All of God's promises to Abraham were ultimately fulfilled in Christ (Galatians 3:14, 16, 29).[15] Before his death, Abraham "began to see God working His purposes through Isaac. In a way it could be said that Abraham saw the Messiah's day: through faith he saw it and was overjoyed (John 8:56)."[16]

God could swear by none greater, so He swore by Himself. Abraham could either accept or reject God's promise. He chose to accept it and was blessed after he endured. Abraham's faith, just like our faith, had to be tested. He faithfully endured and became the father of the faithful (James 2:21ff.).

By noting the example of Abraham, we are reminded that faith is not merely a NT concept, but one that is demonstrated throughout the scriptures. Habakkuk teaches, "The just shall live by faith" (Habakkuk 2:4). The writer of Hebrews quotes Habakkuk (Hebrews 10:38) and then proceeds to define faith and provide OT examples of those who lived by faith in chapter eleven.

---

[14] Lightfoot, *Jesus Christ Today*, 130.
[15] Ibid.
[16] Ibid.

Accordingly, man is to come to God with conviction, with "full assurance of faith" (Hebrews 10:22), with certainty that He exists and that He rewards (Hebrews 11:6). From the OT we learn that "biblical faith is an assurance, a certainty, in contrast with modern concepts of faith as something possible, hopefully true, but not certain."[17]

NT writers understood the nature of faith as a conviction and a substantial certainty undergirding the hope of the believer. A person must come to God by faith – i.e., with conviction and certainty that He exists and that He rewards. A person must make decisions based upon this conviction – this *faith*. To violate his conviction would be sinful (Romans 14:23). We are saved by faith, but not by faith *alone*. Our conviction and certainty in God must move us to action (James 2:14ff.).

"For men indeed swear by the greater, and an oath for confirmation is for them an end of all dispute" **(6:16)**. Our Lord addressed swearing by the greater in His Sermon on the Mount (Matthew 5:33-37). The Pharisees practiced swearing as a means of enabling a lie. In other words, a lie could be permitted if the liar did not swear. A Christian's word must

---

[17] R. Laird Harris, Archer, and Waltke, *Theological Wordbook of the Old Testament* (Chicago, IL: Moody Publishers, 1980), 51.

carry greater integrity and yield all such swearing pointless. However, even in legal proceedings an oath is still required as the right hand is laid upon "the greater," the word of God.

"Thus God, determining to show more abundantly to the heirs of promise the immutability of His counsel..." **(6:17-18).** The two immutable things are God's promise and His oath. The oath was confirmation of the promise. God's promise would have stood and been fulfilled, regardless of an oath being given, as God cannot lie (Numbers 23:19; Titus 1:2). But, to give encouragement and assurance in the fullest possible way to the heirs of the promise, God ratified His promise with an oath.[18]

By His word, we have a strong consolation and a refuge of hope. His word is sure and steadfast. God's word lives and abides forever. All hope that based on His enduring word (1 Peter 1:25) is considered a "living hope" (1 Peter 1:3).

"This hope we have as an anchor of the soul both sure and steadfast..." **(6:19-20).** The promise made to Abraham was kept in Jesus. Jesus is the promise. Jesus is the hope. Not only does Jesus fulfill God's promise but He gives us an

---

[18] Robert Milligan, *A Commentary on the Epistle to the Hebrews* in the Gospel Advocate Commentary Series (Nashville, TN: Gospel Advocate Company, 1989), 234.

anchor of hope. Our hope can rest fully upon His grace, His word, and His promises (1 Peter 1:13).

Biblical hope is not a blind leap in the dark. It is never based on uncertainty and chance, but always based on God, His character, and His truth. Christians are delivered from the groanings of this life by their hope (Romans 8:24). The hope provided in Christ amounts to a trusting conviction and assurance that God's word will come to pass, God is in control, victory is in Christ, and heaven awaits the faithful.

Entering *"the Presence behind the veil..."* refers to the heavenly Presence of God. The veil was the curtain that separated the holy place from the most holy place, first in the tabernacle and later in the temple. The veil in the temple and the temple itself represented the heavenly reality of the Divine Presence where Christ is now seated at God's right hand. The veil in heaven is *"where the forerunner has entered for us, even Jesus..."* When Jesus was crucified and gave up His spirit to the Father, the veil was rent in the temple, signifying to us that the way was now open to the true Holiest of Holies – God's throne in heaven. We now have access to the very presence of God and His throne of grace through the sacrificial love of our Lord Jesus.

As Aaron and his descendants entered the Most Holy place once per year throughout the years of the Levitical priesthood, Christ entered once into the Divine Presence to remain forever. The subject of the Levitical priesthood was at the heart of Judaism. Strong and convincing arguments would be required by the writer for them to relinquish the hold they had on this facet of their religion. Thus, the writer must prove that only Jesus, *"having become High Priest forever according to the order of Melchizedek,"* is to be considered as our intercessor and advocate with the Father.

The writer began this heartfelt discourse concerning the Lord's priesthood by referring to Jesus as our merciful and faithful High Priest (2:17) and by pleading, "consider Jesus, the Apostle and High Priest of our confession …" (3:1). The plea to consider Jesus properly is the purpose of the sermon and is most assuredly the focus of chapters three through ten. Only a brief exhortation to encourage spiritual maturity is interjected in this portion of the work (5:11-6:19). We see Christ's priesthood for the first time being compared to Melchizedek's in 5:6, and again reiterated in 5:10. The writer picks up this idea again in 6:20 and will carry over the comparison into chapter 7.

Melchizedek is a most interesting person to consider. Very little is said about him and even less is known. He is pictured in history in Genesis 14. 1,000 years later he is mentioned in connection to Christ through a Messianic portion of Psalm 110. Another millennium passed and the One to whom the Psalmist referred appears. The writer of Hebrews mentions Melchizedek far more than the other sacred writers.[19]

The name "Melchizedek" is a compound word. "Melek" is the Hebrew word for "king." Tzedek is Hebrew for "righteous." His authority was not vested in human ancestry but in his relationship with the Most High. He is set forth as a type of Christ. Christ is not set forth as a type of Melchizedek. It may be that the personal history of Melchizedek is closed to us for this reason. He is a type of the Son of God. In a book full of genealogies, none is provided for Melchizedek, only an uninterrupted office and timeless priesthood is to be suggested. The fact that Melchizedek appears as he does is a foretaste of the coming Christ and the nature of His Person and Priesthood.

---

[19] Morgan, *God's Last Word to Man*, 80ff.

"For this Melchizedek, king of Salem, priest of the Most High God, who met Abraham returning from the slaughter of the kings and blessed him…" **(7:1).** As noted, the history of Melchizedek is certainly mysterious to say the least. He suddenly appeared on the scene after "The Battle of the Kings" (Genesis 14:1-11). Upon Abraham's return from rescuing Lot (Genesis 14:12-17), he is met by Melchizedek (v.18). Two things happen in this meeting: (1) Melchizedek blesses Abraham (v.19); (2) Abraham pays tithes to Melchizedek (v.20 b). In Hebrews 7:1-2 we have a summary of the events of Genesis 14, and an explanation of Melchizedek's name and title. Note, *"to whom also Abraham gave a tenth part of all, first being translated 'king of righteousness,' and then also king of Salem, meaning 'king of peace'"* **(7:2).** The facts given by the writer have stimulated the interest of many through the years as to the identity of Melchizedek. Some have claimed that he was an angel; Noah's son Shem; Enoch; and even a pre-incarnate appearance of Christ. Bible students have remained intrigued by the description of Melchizedek being *"without father, without mother, without genealogy, having neither beginning of days nor end of life, but made like the Son of God, remains a priest continually"* **(7:3).**

Before we go too far in theorizing, we must ask what is being said by the writer. Is he saying that Melchizedek had no father, mother, beginning, or end? If so, then many speculations will continue to abound. But, if the writer is stating that there is no *scriptural* testimony of Melchizedek's father, mother, beginning, or end, then our conclusion can be narrowed. The significance of this omission of Melchizedek's lineage proves to us that he was *not* made a priest because of the priestly heritage of the Levites. Neither was Jesus made our High Priest after the order of the Levitical priestly heritage. In fact, Jesus was not even born of the tribe of Levi, but of the tribe of Judah. Melchizedek sets a precedent of someone not having to be a priest after this order when not living under the Old Law, or in the Mosaic Age.

Consider the following similarities between Christ and the forerunner Melchizedek: The word "Melchizedek" meaning "King of righteousness," and the title "King of Salem" meaning "King of peace," aptly describe our King Jesus. Melchizedek was both king and priest, as is Christ. Melchizedek received tithes of Abraham. Christ receives freewill offerings from the seed of Abraham, His church. Melchizedek brought forth bread and wine; the Lord instituted His Supper with bread and wine. Melchizedek blessed

Abraham; Christ continues to bless Abraham's seed. Melchizedek's priesthood interceded for Hebrews and Gentiles. Christ, likewise, is the High Priest of all mankind, making no racial, ethnic, or societal distinctions.

We should also note Psalms 76:2 in this portion of our study, which identifies Jerusalem as **Salem**. Jerusalem means "city of peace" and Salem was likely the abbreviated name of the city during Abraham's lifetime. Moreover, Genesis 14:17 mentions the Valley of Shaveh or "the King's Valley." A "King's Valley" also existed in Jerusalem during the life of David, which is likely the same place (cf. 2 Samuel 18:18). Before the land was possessed by the Israelites, monotheism was being practiced there, and Melchizedek was their king and priest. Modern liberals who claim that monotheism was a Hebrew contribution to humanity, would do well do consider the history of ancient Salem.

"Now consider how great this man was, to whom even the patriarch Abraham gave a tenth of the spoils" **(7:4).** Melchizedek was a great man, even greater than Abraham in his time. Even Abraham paid tithes to Melchizedek. *"And indeed those who are of the sons of Levi...have come from the loins of Abraham..."* **(7:5).** The writer offers the following connection, which is the main point of the argument: if

the Levitical priesthood came through the lineage of Abraham, and Abraham offered tithes to Melchizedek, then the Levites could not have had priority over Melchizedek's priesthood. Furthermore, *"he whose genealogy is not derived from them received tithes from Abraham and blessed him who had the promises. Now beyond all contradiction the lesser is blessed by the better"* (7:6). As with Jesus, Melchizedek did not come from the genealogy of the Levites. The lesser (Abraham) is blessed by the greater (Melchizedek). So too, we who are unworthy, are blessed by the Greater – the Lord Jesus Christ.

"Here mortal men receive tithes, but there he receives them, of whom it is witnessed that he lives" (7:8). The Levites are the mortal men who receive tithes here, which seems to be an indication that the temple in Jerusalem was still standing at the time of the writing. The Levites were mortal men who died. He, Melchizedek, who serves as a symbol for Christ, lives. The writer is continuing his thought from verse 3, concerning Melchizedek who "having neither beginning of days nor end of life, but made like the Son of God, remains a priest continually."

"Even Levi, who receives tithes, paid tithes through Abraham, so to speak..." (7:9-10). The writer concludes that even Levi, while in the loins of Abraham, paid tithes to Melchizedek. In scripture, the name of an ancestor can stand for the whole of his descendants.[20] Levi was Abraham's great-grandson. Levi's priesthood was preceded in greatness by Melchizedek's and superseded in greatness by Christ's. The writer is continuing the line of reasoning which acknowledges the superiority of Christ to everything which preceded Him. Christ is superior to the prophets, angels, Moses, Joshua, and the priesthood of the Aaron.

Christ's priesthood offers perfection to the sinner and completion in the plan of God. *"Therefore, if perfection were through the Levitical priesthood..." (7:11).* The argument of the imperfection of the priesthood and the law it represented is now being introduced and will be explained with greater detail as the book continues. The writer begins this line of reasoning by asking, *"what further need was there that another priest should rise...?"* If the Levitical priesthood was perfect or complete in God's design for human salvation and fulfillment of His promise to Abraham, why did the Psalmist speak of a coming priesthood after the order of Melchizedek (cf. Psalm 110:4)?

---

[20] cf. Jacob, Esau, and even Adam are examples of this possibility of the individual representing the group in a corporate sense.

"For the priesthood being changed, of necessity there is also a change of the law" **(7:12).** The change in the priesthood coincided with the change in the law. We now live under a new law and new priesthood. The coupling of the law and the priesthood will now become a central idea in the letter. The writer states that the priesthood has changed. There are no more priests after the order of Aaron. We are all priests now (1 Peter 2:9), and Christ is our High Priest.

A new priesthood requires a new law. The NT is the covenant law that is now effectual for "every tribe and tongue, people and nation" (Revelation 5:9). The law of Moses was given specifically to the nation of Israel and none other. When God spoke with Moses in the mountaintop of Sinai, He said that His word was to be directed unto "the house of Jacob and the children of Israel" (Exodus 19:3, 5-6). God also spoke to Israel through Jeremiah when the time came to inform them of a new covenant (Jeremiah 31:34).

Moreover, a law only speaks to those who are under it. The law of Moses never spoke to any other nation, including the church. The law was to be preached unto Israel just as the gospel is to be preached unto every creature and nation today. Christ said, "preach the gospel unto every creature" (Mark 16:15), and "teach all nations" (Matthew 28:18-20).

These are two different religious systems for two different groups of people. One system has ceased, and the other system is now in place.

Jesus Christ gave the gospel, the new covenant, as a spiritual law to speak to every nation, people, kindred, and tongue of the earth. The gospel, not the law of Moses, has been ordained by God to be the universal covenant between God and man. Just as Israel was peculiar (special) to God in that system, Christians are peculiar (special) to God in the gospel system (1 Peter 2:9).

The law was limited in its recipients, its purpose, and its duration. The law could not perfect the conscience (Hebrews 9:9) because it could never fully satisfy our sin debt (Hebrews 10:1). We now have a better covenant, which has been established on better promises (Hebrews 8:6-7). Man is now saved by the gospel (Romans 1:16-17). God has promised and given a new covenant (Hebrews 8:8-12). Man must now obey the gospel of Christ – not the Law of Moses – if he is to be saved.

"For He of whom these things are spoken belongs to another tribe, from which no man has officiated at the altar" (7:13). Christ did not come from the tribe of Levi, but

the tribe of Judah.[21] "For *it is* evident that our Lord arose from Judah, of which tribe Moses spoke nothing concerning priesthood" (7:14). The writer is not urging his readers to accept Christ on the basis of Levitical heritage, but on the basis of His being a High Priest over an entirely new and different priesthood of all believers. Thus, Christ's credentials as High Priest do not follow those given to Aaron, and "not according to the law of a fleshly commandment, but according to the power of an endless life" (7:15-16). He argues thusly, once again quoting from Psalm 110:4, "For He testifies: 'You *are* a priest forever according to the order of Melchizedek'" (7:17).

"For on the one hand there is an annulling of the former commandment because of its weakness and unprofitableness..." (7:18-19). The writer continues his argument of the imperfection of the law. He will continue by stating that the law was never able to cleanse the conscience as it was never able to take away sins. There was always a remembrance of sin under the law, as the writer of Hebrews will soon say (Hebrews 10:1-4).

---

[21] cf. Genesis 49:8-12; Matthew 1:1-6; Luke 3:31-34; Revelation 5:5-6

Not even the most faithful under the law of Moses were cleansed by those offerings. These dear souls were, however, ultimately forgiven by the blood of Christ (Romans 3:24-26). The writer will also add, "And for this reason He is the Mediator of the new covenant, by means of death, for the redemption of the transgressions under the first covenant, that those who are called may receive the promise of the eternal inheritance" (Hebrews 9:15).

The blood of Christ was shed for the redemption of all the faithful under the first covenant as well as all the faithful under the new covenant. No soul can be saved from sin, in any age, except by the blood of Christ. We will find this also later in Hebrews (Hebrews 10:10-12).

"And inasmuch as He was not made priest without an oath..." **(7:20-22).** Just as God kept His word to Abraham (Hebrews 6:13ff.), He has kept His word concerning Christ. Christ is High Priest according to the oath made by the Father. A better covenant has been inaugurated by this oath. Christ came to fulfill the law (Matthew 5:17-18). The door of opportunity for a covenant with all people has been opened. Christ established His kingdom in which His law governs, and His grace forgives (cf. Ephesians 2:11-16).

The law has been nailed to the cross (Colossians 2:14) – including ceremonial laws such as the Sabbath (Colossians 2:17). By His death and the coming of the NT, Christ made the OT "old" (Hebrews 8:13). Christ took away the first so that He could establish the second (Hebrews 10:9). God caused the Law of Moses "to be done away...abolished...in Christ" (2 Corinthians 3:6-18). Christ is now the High Priest over the house of God (Hebrews 4:4-16), which is the household of faith (Galatians 6:10).

"Also there were many priests..." (7:24). During the OT period, there were many priests who came and went. The priesthood of Christ is eternal and continues forever; it is unchanging and will only ever have one High Priest officiating. It is furthermore distinguished from the Levitical priesthood in these ways. The priesthood of Christ according to the pattern set forth by God also nullifies any attempt to recreate a "Christian" version of the Levitical priesthood. The only High Priest the church will ever know is Jesus Christ. The only High Priest the church will ever need is Jesus Christ.

"Therefore He is also able to save to the uttermost..." (7:25). Tremendous assurance is given to the saints in this verse. Christ's intercession depends on two things – He must be willing, and He must be able. His willingness to intercede

was expressed in terms of His sympathy in Hebrews 4:15. His ability was first expressed in 2:18, as "He is able to aid those who are tempted." The verse under our consideration currently presents and/or affirms five great truths pertaining to the priesthood and intercession of Christ.

Frist, Christ is *able*. When man is unable, helpless, and hopeless in weakness, God through Christ is able.

- ….and being fully convinced that what He had promised He was also able to perform (Romans 4:21).
- Who are you to judge another's servant? To his own master he stands or falls. Indeed, he will be made to stand, for God is able to make him stand (Romans 14:4).
- Now to Him who is able to establish you according to my gospel and the preaching of Jesus Christ, according to the revelation of the mystery kept secret since the world began (Romans 16:25).
- And God is able to make all grace abound toward you, that you, always having all sufficiency in all things, may have an abundance for every good work (2 Corinthians 9:8).
- Now to Him who is able to do exceedingly abundantly above all that we ask or think, according to the power that works in us, to Him be glory in the church by Christ

Jesus to all generations, forever and ever. Amen (Ephesians 3:20-21).

- Now to Him who is able to keep you from stumbling, And to present you faultless before the presence of His glory with exceeding joy (Jude 24).

Once again, in Hebrews we find that Christ is able to aid those who are tempted (Hebrews 2:18). Consequently, He is able to save to the uttermost those who draw near to God through Him (Hebrews 7:25). In each of these points, man is unable, but God is able.

Secondly, He *saves to the uttermost*. Christ has promised that He will not cast out any who come to Him. Man must come by faith, repentance, and obedience. If man will approach Christ as Christ has commanded, he will find Him to be a faithful and merciful Savior. Christ has promised to save "whosoever wills" of every nation, kindred, people, and tongue of the earth. The young and old can come to Jesus. The rich and the poor will find Him. He is the crucified Savior of the world, and by the grace of God has tasted death for every man (Hebrews 2:9).

Thirdly, man can *come to God through Him*. The way to the Most Holy place in heaven is open and man can approach the throne of God through Him (4:16). Man needs no other, only Christ (cf. 1 Timothy 2:5; 1 John 2:1, 2).

Paul wrote to Timothy and affirmed, "For there is one God and one Mediator between God and men, the Man Christ Jesus, who gave Himself a ransom for all, to be testified in due time" (1 Timothy 2:5-6). It is absurd to believe that Mary, any departed saint, or so-called priest, pastor, or prophet was ever intended to serve in this capacity. Paul said there is *one* mediator, and that mediator is Christ.

The apostle John wrote, "My little children, these things I write to you, that you may not sin. And if anyone sins, we have an Advocate with the Father, Jesus Christ the righteous" (1 John 2:1). John said that our Advocate is Jesus Christ the righteous, not Mary, Muhammad, Joseph Smith, or anyone else.

The writer began this document by affirming, "when He had by Himself purged our sins, sat down at the right hand of the Majesty on high" (1:3). He will add later, "But this Man, after He had offered one sacrifice for sins forever, sat down at the right hand of God" (10:12). And, "For by one offering He has perfected forever those who are being sanctified" (10:14). Only one sacrifice for sin will count. Only one way to the Father exists. He will forever be "the way, the truth, and the life, and no man can come to the Father except through Him" (John 14:6).

Fourthly, He remains and will always remain *alive*. Paul wrote, "For if when we were enemies we were reconciled to God through the death of His Son, much more, having been reconciled, we shall be saved by His life" (Romans 5:10). If God loved man so greatly to reconcile him to Himself when he was an enemy to God by the death of Christ, how much more will God love and bless man through the eternal life of Christ? Christ is going nowhere. He will never experience death again. Unlike the Levitical priesthood, which had priests come and go by virtue of their own mortality, Jesus remains alive. Man will never again have another High Priest. Man will never need another High Priest. Man should never want another High Priest!

Lastly, He makes intercession *for them*. The ones in covenant relationship with God through Christ have the promise of intercession. Those outside or those who have left Christ, have no promise of intercession. Without Christ, man is without God and without hope (Ephesians 2:12ff.).

"For such a High Priest was fitting for us..." (7:26-27). Consider the characteristics of Christ stated in these two verses. (1) He is fitting. (2) He is holy. (3) He is undefiled. (4) He is separate from sinners. (5) He is higher than the heavens. (6) He needs no sacrifice for His own sins. (7) He does not offer His sacrifice daily, but once for all. (8) He offered up Himself. *"For the law appoints as high priests men who have weakness..."* (7:28).

God's oath, found in Psalm 110:4, concerning Christ being made a High Priest after the order of Melchizedek, came after the law was given. Christ has been appointed by the oath. He has been perfected forever. Christians are complete in Christ. "For in Him dwells all the fullness of the Godhead bodily; and you are complete in Him, who is the head of all principality and power" (Colossians 2:9-10). By His resurrection, God has made Jesus our Lord and Christ (Acts 2:36). He has all power or authority in heaven and in earth and we are to obey Him (Matthew 28:18, 20). Jesus Christ "is the blessed and only Potentate, the King of kings and Lord of lords" (1 Timothy 6:15).

Hebrews 7 provides several superior distinctions of Christ's priesthood to the priesthood of Aaron.

1.) There is only one High Priest, Jesus. He will never die or be replaced. He *ever lives* to make intercession for us. Jesus abides forever. So too does His word (1 Peter 1:22-25). So too will everyone who lives by His word (1 John 2:15-17).

2.) His priesthood is unchangeable. It is perfect and therefore will never need any changes.

3.) He can save to the uttermost every person that comes to Him. He will never be unable to save someone that comes to Him.

4.) He is holy, blameless, undefiled, separate from sinners, and higher than the heavens. No Levitical priest could ever make such a claim.

5.) He does not need a sacrifice for His own sin, for He kept the law perfectly (also read Galatians 3:13ff.). He offers His perfect sacrifice solely on behalf of the people forevermore. His blood is powerful enough to cleanse every sin committed by every person (1 John 1:7-2:2).

Summary

The law, including its priesthood, was added because of Israel's transgressions, and served as a tutor to bring them to Christ. Foreseeing the end of the law and the ratification of the new covenant by the blood of Christ, God gave an oath concerning Him to make Christ the High Priest over the house of God (the blood-bought church) after the order of Melchizedek.

The law offered life to anyone who could keep it perfectly, but no man could, save one – Jesus Christ. Thus, the law became a curse to the Jews because of their failure to keep it perfectly and thus find justification therein. But Christ, who kept it perfectly, took the curse of the law away by His sacrifice for our sins, "hanging on the tree," bringing redemption and justification for the sins the law could not touch.

Our Lord was not ordained as High Priest according to the law, but by Divine appointment from the Father. Melchizedek's priesthood prefigured the priesthood of Christ. The Levitical priesthood served as an interim priesthood to bring Israel to the atonement and intercession provided in their Messiah. In Christ, the fulfillment of God's plan for man's mediation is realized and perfected.

Section Four
The Ministry of Christ as High Priest
8:1 – 10:18

"Now this is the main point of the things we are saying: We have such a High Priest, who is seated at the right hand of the throne of the Majesty in the heavens, a Minister of the sanctuary and of the true tabernacle which the Lord erected, and not man" **(8:1-2).** The fact and nature of the priesthood of Christ has been discussed up to this point in Hebrews. In the forthcoming chapters, the actual function of His work as High Priest will be taught in greater detail. Or, if you will, chapters 5-7 have dealt with the *person* of Christ as our High Priest. Chapters 8-10 will present to us the *ministry* of Christ as High Priest.

In chapter 7 we learned that a change of the law was necessitated by the change of the priesthood (7:12). We learned that a certain "weakness and unprofitableness" was evident in the law (7:18). We were told to look for a "better hope" (7:19) which is made sure by a "better testament" (7:22). We now have an "unchangeable priesthood" (7:24) with an unchangeable High Priest (13:8) ever living to make intercession for us (7:25).

In chapter 8:1, we see that the writer is about to summarize what he has been saying about Christ's priesthood by the phrase, "this is the main point." Not only does the opening sentence of this chapter serve as a concluding statement for the previous thought of Christ as High Priest, but it also serves as an introduction statement for the next theme, which is the ministry of our High Priest. The location of His ministry as High Priest is in heaven where He is *"seated at the right hand of the throne of the Majesty in the heavens."* The heavenly Most Holy Place, in the presence of God, is the only place where sin can be atoned, and man can be reconciled to God.

The writer provides his readers with insight concerning the throne room of God, describing it as *"the true tabernacle which the Lord erected, and not man."* From this statement we learn the value of types and shadows in the OT. The rituals, practices, offices, and edifices of the Old Law foreshadowed what was going to occur in the NT. The tabernacle and later the temple was an earthly representation of a heavenly reality. The priesthood foreshadowed the church – a priesthood of all believers with the High Priest being Christ. The altar foreshadowed the cross where the sacrifice for sin is made. The laver for washing foreshadowed baptism where man is sanctified and cleansed with the washing of water by the word. The door to the tabernacle prefigures the way provided by Christ. The veil in the temple typified the barrier of sin. It was opened at the crucifixion when it was rent from top to bottom as though hands reached down from heaven to tear it. The Holiest Place typified God's throne in heaven itself.

The fact that these earthly things were clearly seen served as a shadow revealing to us the reality of the heavenly substance (see Colossians 2:17). If there is a shadow, there must be something causing the shadow to be cast. The shadow was cast on earth from the presence of these things in heaven. Such detail was given to the "shadow" according to their pattern or instruction because of the heavenly realities these things represented (see Exodus 25ff.).

"For every high priest is appointed to offer both gifts and sacrifices. Therefore it is necessary that this One also have something to offer…" (8:3-5). The work of a priest is to offer gifts and sacrifices to God on behalf of men. "The

fundamental idea of sacrifice in the Old Testament is that of substitution, which again seems to imply everything else – atonement and redemption, vicarious punishment and forgiveness."[1] The readers needed to see Jesus as High Priest and that He offered Himself to provide a perfect atonement or *covering* for our sins (cf. Psalm 32:1-2).[2]

Notice the phrase *"Therefore it is necessary"* concerning Christ's gift as it should impress us with the absolute importance of a particular matter. Christ offered Himself so that every man would be offered the opportunity to be reconciled to God (cf. 2 Corinthians 5:18-21). Christ offered His gift of salvation according to the blessed will of His Father. The "offering" whereof the writer speaks is truly heaven's gift to man.

***"But now He has obtained a more excellent ministry, inasmuch as He is also Mediator of a better covenant, which was established on better promises"* (8:3-6).** In Hebrews 8:6 we find the summary of His priesthood provided through a three-fold description: (1) a more excellent minis-

---

[1] Alfred Edersheim, *The Temple: Its Ministry and Services* (Peabody, MA: Hendrickson Publishers, 1994), 76.
[2] Ibid.

try; (2) a better covenant; and (3) better promises. From Hebrews 8:7–10:31, we are going to learn the significance of this new covenant. In this portion of scripture, we have perhaps the most detailed examination of the NT replacing the OT in the Bible.

Christ's ministry, covenant, and promise emphasizes the superiority of His priesthood. The term "covenant" denotes an agreement made between two or more parties. In this relationship, it is God who issues the terms of the covenant. Only when man accepts His covenant will he be blessed by His spiritual promises. As sinners, our concern should be to understand *how* man is saved by God's grace and *when* man's sins are atoned by the blood of Christ. God is offering grace, mercy, and help to those who believe, repent, and obey Him. Herein we find the basis for God's covenantal relationship with man. When man obeys God, he is accepting the gift of God's grace – i.e., the atonement of His only-begotten Son. If man refuses to obey God, he is rejecting the gift of God's grace; he is rejecting Christ.

"For if that first covenant had been faultless, then no place would have been sought for a second." The first covenant being the covenant God made with Israel, was imperfect. The second covenant – the new covenant of Christ – is

perfect. The law of Moses was limited in its recipients, its purpose, and its duration. The law could not perfect the conscience (Hebrews 9:9), because it could never fully satisfy our sin debt (Hebrews 10:1). We now have a better covenant, which has been established on better promises (Hebrews 8:6-7).

"Because finding fault with them, He says: 'Behold, the days are coming, says the Lord, when I will make a new covenant...'" **(vv. 8-13).** The writer here quotes from and applies the fulfillment of Jeremiah 31:31-34. The Lord found fault with the first covenant as this law was not intended to last until the end of the world. Neither was it intended to take away sins and could not, therefore, cleanse the conscience of sin. Moreover, as we have learned, the priesthood of Aaron could not compare with the priesthood of Christ.

The first covenant was also imperfect in that it did not encompass all of humanity in its precepts. The law was given to Israel because of their transgressions in the wilderness (Galatians 3:19) to serve as a teacher/tutor/schoolmaster to bring them to the point of faith in Christ (Galatians 3:24). From the beginning, God had determined to bring Christ into the world through the seed/line of Abraham to bless all nations (Genesis 12:3).

So that Israel would have a moral compass to guide them until the time of Christ, God gave them the law. Now that Christ has come, fulfilled that law (Matthew 5:17-18), and nailed it to His cross (Colossians 2:14), the time has come for the new covenant to be given. This new covenant is the "second" of which the writer speaks.

The new covenant was made with the house of Israel and Judah. When Jeremiah spoke these words, Israel had been divided into two kingdoms – north and south. Also remember that the gospel was first preached to the Jews (Acts 1-9) and later to the Gentiles (Acts 10-28), beginning with Cornelius (Acts 10). The new covenant was not going to be according to the old covenant. It would be an altogether different law to govern a different people (the church). The writer recalls that Israel chose not to continue in that covenant, and therefore, the Lord "disregarded them." As we have been studying, this principle is true with the new covenant as well.

The new covenant would not be given on tables of stone, but by God working, revealing, and speaking through the minds and hearts of those He inspired (v.10). The Holy Spirit guided the apostles into all truth (John 16:13). He did not do this all at once, to any one individual. Rather, He revealed to the "inner man" of His apostles the things of the Spirit (1

Corinthians 2:1ff.). The promise of a covenant relationship given to the recipients of the NT was the same as was given to the Israelites in the OT – "I will be their God and they shall be My people."

Another way the new differs from the old is the way one enters the covenant. *"None of them shall teach his neighbor, and none his brother, saying, 'Know the Lord,' for all shall know Me, from the least of them to the greatest of them"* **(10:11).** A Jew became a Jew when circumcised on the eighth day, although he did not know why. He was taught to know the Lord *after* he had already been sealed with the seal of that covenant.

The new covenant does not work that way. (Understanding this point will give you a strong reason to reject infant baptism). According to the new covenant, one must be taught *before* entering this relationship with God. "Faith comes by hearing and hearing by the word of God" (Romans 10:17). The gospel must be preached and obeyed for a person to enter the new covenant. Therefore, "all shall know me." All those in this covenant will know the Lord and why they are in this covenant. Such knowledge will not come after the fact.

Moreover, no longer will a person be physically born into a covenant with God. That is not to say that infants are not pure and innocent. We accept the fact that they have not committed any transgression, for there must be knowledge before transgression (see Isaiah 7:15-16; Romans 7:9). However, this simply means that a person cannot be physically born as a Christian. For this to occur they must be born again (John 3:3-5).

An added promise of the new covenant is one that was not provided in the old covenant – *"their sins and their iniquities will I remember no more."* The Israelites had an annual Day of Atonement to offer sacrifice for sins already committed, hence their sins were still remembered. The Christian's Day of Atonement came at the cross when God made "Him who knew no sin to be made sin for us."

The writer also teaches us how the OT became "old." The answer: ***"In that He says, 'A new covenant,' He has made the first obsolete. Now what is becoming obsolete and growing old is ready to vanish away"*** **(8:13).** The reason why we call the OT "old" is because God has made it *old* by giving us something *new*. The final thought of this chapter concerns the old decaying and being ready to vanish away, which seems to be another statement indicating that temple services were still being practiced at the time of this writing. This service did vanish away, never to be established again.

"Then indeed, even the first covenant had ordinances of divine service and the earthly sanctuary" (9:1). Chapter 9 begins where chapter 8 concluded. The thought that links the two chapters is the covenant of Christ compared to the covenant of Moses. In chapter 8:7-13 we read several ways the new covenant was different from the old. In the first verse of chapter nine, the writer introduces the idea of "regulations of divine worship" (NASB). While we have certain regulations in the NT, they are clearly different from the regulations which governed the Israelites.

The Jews had an "elaborate and particular" system which regulated the admission, services, and privileges of the officiating priesthood.[3] The first regulation stated pertains to the tabernacle (9:2). Within the tabernacle, and later the temple, were two rooms separated by a veil (a large curtain the height and width of the inner part of the structure). The first room was called the Holy Place. The inner room, behind the veil,

---

[3] Edersheim, *The Temple*, 73. Edersheim continues his thought adding, "Yet it has all vanished, not leaving behind it in the synagogue even a single trace of its complicated and perfect arrangements. These 'old things are passed away,' because they were only 'a shadow of good things to come.' But 'the substance is of Christ,' and 'He abideth an High-Priest for ever.'"

was called the Most Holy Place or Holy of Holies. The earthly tabernacle was made according to the pattern (8:5) and divine ordinances were set forth by God. In Hebrews 9:2-5, the Hebrew writer gives his readers a brief description of the contents of the tabernacle.

Some difficulty may arise in the study of verse 4 and the topic of the golden censer. According to the writer the censer was in the second of the two compartments of the tabernacle, the "Holiest of all." The difficulty is that Moses placed the censer in the "holy place," the first compartment (Exodus 40:26-27). An explanation can be found in Leviticus 16:12-13. In this passage we see that the high priest was to take the censer into the "Holiest of all" on the Day of Atonement. Notice, *"And he shall take a censer full of burning coals of fire from off the altar before the Lord, and his hands full of sweet incense beaten small, **and bring it within the veil**..."* It seems that the censer could be found in both places depending on when you were looking for it.[4]

The two compartments were separated by the veil which was torn from top to bottom during our Lord's crucifixion

---

[4] Another possibility is that the censor stood at the entrance to the Most Holy Place and its smoke filled both rooms. In this case, the censor is being described more in terms of function than in terms of actual location (McClister, 299).

(cf. Matthew 27:51). The tearing of the veil signifies to us that God from heaven has provided a way of entry into the Holiest of all – literally heaven itself – through the sacrifice of Christ (cf. Hebrews 6:19; 10:20). Every Christian can approach the true mercy seat of God by the blood of Christ (see Hebrews 4:16ff.).

"Now when these things had been thus prepared..." **(9:6-10).** In Hebrews 9:6-10, a comparison made is between the priest and the high priest of the earthly tabernacle (vv.6-7). The number of priests at the time of writing, especially in Jerusalem, is believed to have been very great.[5] But there was only one high priest. From the beginning of the priesthood, the high priest was elevated to a greater degree of importance. He was exclusively ordained to enter within the veil into the "Holiest of all" to make an offering for his sins as well as the sins of the people (v.7; Leviticus 16). The annual sacrifices under the law were to be maintained on the Day of Atonement as an offering for the sins of the high priest and the sins of the people. The writer continues the comparison by explaining, "the Holy Spirit indicating this, that the way into the Holiest of All was not yet made mani-

---

[5] Edersheim, 56.

fest while the first tabernacle was still standing. It was symbolic for the present time in which both gifts and sacrifices are offered which cannot make him who performed the service perfect in regard to the conscience…" (9:9-10).

The actions of the priests were done to signify a greater lesson: that these things were being done as a figure of the true tabernacle (see also Hebrews 8:2). The Holiest of all had not yet been literally manifested. God's eternal plan for His people had yet to be enacted. The temporary tabernacle was just that, temporary. Perfection or completion of God's plan was yet to come and was not a thing to be attained during the time of the tabernacle. "Now we see what our author wishes to teach his readers. The really effective barrier to a man's free access to God is an inward and not a material one; it exists in his conscience. It is only when the conscience is purified that a man is set free to approach God without reservation and offer Him acceptable service and worship."[6]

The writer will once again amplify the greater glory of Christ. His readers are left virtually on the edge of their seat, wanting to know what would bring perfection. The stage is now set for the writer's comments on the Lord's sacrifice

---

[6] Bruce, 196.

and the fulfilled atonement for the sins of the people to occur at "the time of reformation" (9:10).

The significance of the tabernacle should not be lost on the readers. The writer has already spoken of the "true tabernacle which the Lord pitched and not man" (8:2); and that such OT examples served as a "shadow of heavenly things" (8:5). Beginning in Hebrews 9:11, we learn how this tabernacle foreshadowed a great "heavenly" truth. As Matthew Henry has well-said, the first tabernacle, "was a dark dispensation, and but for a short continuance, only designed for a while to typify the great things of Christ and the gospel, that were in due time to shine forth in their own brightness, and thereby cause all the shadows to flee away and disappear, as the stars before the rising sun."[7]

The writer of Hebrews continues, *"But Christ came as High Priest of the good things to come..."* (9:11). As an earthly high priest enters an earthly tabernacle, our heavenly High Priest entered a heavenly tabernacle. He entered within the veil and broke down that barrier of sin so that we may go before the very throne of God with confidence. Jesus' concern was not merely for "foods and drinks, various washings,

---

[7] Henry, 746.

and fleshly ordinances" (9:10). *But* Christ came concerning "good things to come." The "good things to come" are all the spiritual blessings found in Christ (Ephesians 1:3).

The greatest themes of the Bible are not only associated with Christ, but they stem from Christ and flow to Christ. Fulfillment and meaning are to be found in Christ. One cannot truthfully consider love, atonement, redemption, reconciliation, justification, sanctification, forgiveness, hope, faithfulness, the resurrection, or eternal life without considering Jesus. He not only taught these great themes, but He personifies them. He is them. These themes come to life through His life and example.

He did not enter heaven *"with the blood of goats and calves, but with His own blood..."* (9:12). Three comparisons pertaining to Christ's sacrifice are made in this statement. (1) The blood by which Christ entered was not the blood of goats and calves, but His own blood; (2) Christ only had to enter the holy place once as compared to the annual entrance of the earthly high priest; and (3) the blood of Christ provides eternal redemption.

It was impossible for the blood of bulls and goats to take away sins. Contrariwise, His sacrifice is perfect and will never have to be made again. His redemption is eternal. He died once and for all (Romans 6:10) to obtain eternal redemption for *us*. Two things to consider from this statement include (1) the meaning of redemption; and (2) that He did it for *us*. To redeem means to "buy back." Redemption is a very significant term as it implies that we once belonged to God. Every person born into this world is born in the light of Christ (John 1:9). Paul stated that he was alive (spiritually) apart from the law (his knowledge of the law), but when the commandment came (his knowledge thereof) sin revived (became alive) and he died (spiritually) (Romans 7:9).

Before a child knows to "refuse the evil and choose the good" (Isaiah 7:15-16), that child is alive spiritually and not held accountable for sins. One must have knowledge of good and evil before sin can come (James 4:17). But, with such knowledge comes the realization that a person has sinned against God (James 1:13-15). When this occurs, the person dies spiritually (cf. Ezekiel 18:19-24; Isaiah 59:1-2). "The wages of sin is death" (Romans 6:23).

Being in a spiritually dead state (Ephesians 2:1ff.), the only way back to God (redemption) is through the reconciliation provided by Christ (2 Corinthians 5:17-21). Christ obtained this eternal redemption for *us*. We are beneficiaries of the greatest inheritance ever known to man, the gift of redemption and reconciliation. Christ provides this gift "by His own blood" (cf. Ephesians 1:7; Revelation 1:5). We could not and cannot redeem our souls. His blood is the only payment God will accept to recover the soul lost in sin. Without Christ, man will die in his sins (John 8:24).

"For if the blood of bulls and goats and the ashes of a heifer, sprinkling the unclean, sanctifies for the purifying of the flesh," (as the Jews believed under the law) *"how much more shall the blood of Christ, who through the eternal Spirit offered Himself without spot to God, cleanse your conscience from dead works to serve the living God?"* **(9:13-14).** The comparison between the sacrifices of bulls and goats and the blood of Christ continues. Note the question, "How much more?" How much more does one have with Christ as compared to without Him? How much more does a soul have in fellowship with Christ when compared to outside of His fellowship? How much more hope does he have? How much more grace does he know? How much more is the peace he possesses – the peace that Christ left for us, the peace that passes understanding? How much more is the sweetness of life and the meaning of love? How much

more will it *cleanse the conscience from dead works to serve the living God!*

The offering of Christ was (1) *preeminent* (much more, greater than all other sacrifices); (2) *predetermined* (through the eternal Spirit); (3) *personal* (He offered Himself); (4) *pure* (without spot); (5) *pleasing* (to God).

"And for this reason He is the Mediator of the new covenant..." (9:15). The covenant of Christ is made effectual because of His death. He alone is the Mediator of this covenant (cf. 1 Timothy 2:5; 1 John 2:1-2). By His blood, all those who were faithful under the first covenant received the promise of everlasting life just like those who are faithful under the new covenant (cf. Romans 3:19-25). Any soul that will be redeemed on the day of final judgment will be redeemed by the blood of Christ. Certainly, this would have been a comforting and even clarifying statement to these Hebrew readers who could have possibly had questions concerning the salvation of their faithful fathers.

In Hebrews 8:18, the writer spoke of the "weakness and unprofitableness" of the law. In Hebrews 9:7, he alluded that the law was not "faultless." Herein, we learn one of the chief weaknesses and faults of the law – its sacrifices could not purify the conscience. There remained a remembrance of sins year after year (Hebrews 10:1). Jesus lifted that curse and brought to us forgiveness of sins once and for all (Hebrews 10:12-14). The gospel of the kingdom was preached in promise before His death and in reality after His death. It was not until Pentecost (Acts 2) that the Old Testament prophecies pertaining to Christ's kingdom were fulfilled.[8]

"For where there is a testament, there must also of necessity be the death of the testator..." **(9:16-17).** It was necessary for Christ to die for His covenant to come "in force" and have "power/authority." To illustrate his point about the new covenant becoming effectual at Christ's death, the writer reminds his Jewish readers of how things were sanctified according to the first covenant by blood. *"Therefore not even the first covenant was dedicated without blood..."* **(9:18-21).**

In the OT, blood was to be *shed and applied* before anything could be counted as clean (see Exodus 24:1-8). Thus, *according to the law almost all things are purified with blood, and without shedding of blood there is no remission"* **(9:22).** Leviticus 17:11 is quoted here to remind the

---

[8] See Isaiah 2:1-4; Joel 2:28; Daniel 2:44; Luke 24:46-47; Mark 9:1; Acts 1:8; Acts 2:1-4

readers of the sacrificial significance of the shedding of blood. Leviticus 17:11 teaches three principles about blood: (1) in the human body, "the life is in the blood;" (2) atonement cannot be made without blood; and (3) without the shedding of blood there is no forgiveness of sin.

The reader is drawn again to the superiority of the blood of Christ and His redemption. Through their various offerings the Israelites obtained a "cleansing of the flesh" (Hebrews 10:13), but never of the conscience. Only the blood of Jesus can cleanse the conscience. Only in His new covenant is the promise fulfilled that "I will remember their sins no more."

The shedding of blood in the OT was intended to serve as a shadow or copy of the heavenly reality of Christ's sacrifice. The death of Christ cast its shadow back upon the OT and was presented to Israel through the offerings for sin made upon the altar. ***"Therefore it was necessary that the copies of the things in the heavens should be purified with these, but the heavenly things themselves with better sacrifices than these" (9:23).*** The rites of purification under the law served as a temporary and instructive way of approaching God in anticipation of Christ's heavenly way of intercession.[9]

"For Christ has not entered the holy places made with hands, which are copies of the true, but into heaven itself, now to appear in the presence of God for us" **(9:24)**. The writer has just made a point concerning shedding and applying blood in the OT. The patterns, types, and shadows found in the OT needed to be purified by blood as they represented heavenly realities and truths to be revealed in Christ. They were initiated according to their Divine pattern for this reason. Every aspect of tabernacle worship was commanded that Christ might be prefigured in them.

Jesus does not appear before His Father with His blood "often" or "every year" as the high priests (9:25). Otherwise, He would be required to be offered just as often here on earth, even from the beginning of the world (9:26). Instead, He came to earth "once at the end of the ages...to put away

---

[9] Peterson, *Hebrews*, 217.

sin by the sacrifice of Himself" (9:26). Two truths are implied from the text: (1) Christ is eternal; and (2) His blood reaches backward to cover the sins of past generations.[10]

"And as it is appointed for men to die once, but after this the judgment, so Christ was offered once to bear the sins of many. To those who eagerly wait for Him He will appear a second time, apart from sin, for salvation" (9:27-28). Just as it is appointed for mankind to die once, Jesus died once. After we die, we face judgment. Man does not return to earth to live again or enjoy a second opportunity to make things right with God. Jesus also died once for sins and will not ever return to address that need again.

He is coming "a second time" (9:28), but not to make an offering for sin. We look for Him to appear a second time "apart from sin," or if you will, apart from making a sacrifice for sin. He is returning "for salvation." When He returns, it will not be to re-live the agony of the cross, but destroy to works of the devil ultimately, defeat death forever, and gather His church to their heavenly reward (cf. 1 Corinthians 15:23ff.).

---

[10] Lightfoot, 176.

At this present time, Jesus rules over all heaven and earth. All authority has been given to Him by the Father (Matthew 28:18; 1 Corinthians 15:27). The government of His kingdom now rests upon His shoulders (Isaiah 9:6). When Jesus returns, He will gather the kingdom – those living and dead – and deliver it to the Father (Matthew 13:24-30; 36-43; 1 Corinthians 15:23-28). The purpose of His return is not to die for sin or to initiate, found, or establish His kingdom. He is coming to gather it. He will summon a universal resurrection of the dead in which all – both good and evil – will come forth (John 5:28-29). He will then make a judgment upon humankind (Matthew 16:26-27; 1 Corinthians 3:13; 2 Timothy 4:1; Jude 14-15) and bring the kingdom into its heavenly and eternal fulfillment (Matthew 25:34).

The world will be destroyed at His coming (Hebrews 1:10-11; 2 Peter 3:10-13). The only kingdom to be spared at His coming will be His kingdom (Hebrews 12:26-29). Christ's return signifies the end of this world (1 Corinthians 15:24). It will be the final event of this world.

Mercy and pardon will cease to be granted as He will come taking vengeance on those who do not know God and have not obeyed His gospel (2 Thessalonians 1:7-9). His coming will bring judgment (Matthew 25:31-46; John 5:26-

29; Revelation 20:11-15). The devil's torment upon man will end and his punishment will begin (Matthew 25:41; Revelation 20:10). The righteous will enter the place prepared for them (John 14:1-3; Hebrews 13:14; Revelation 14:13). The wicked will be cast from the presence of God into the lake that burns with fire and brimstone (Revelation 20:14-15; 21:8; 22:15) to suffer for eternity in hell (Matthew 25:46; Revelation 14:11). The certainty of these events cannot be successfully denied. "He will appear." He said Himself, "I will come again." We must watch and be ready for we do not know the hour only the certainty of our Lord's return.

"For the law, having a shadow of the good things to come, and not the very image of the things, can never with these same sacrifices, which they offer continually year by year, make those who approach perfect" **(10:1).** The law and the ordinances contained therein served as a shadow of good things to come. A Shadow is only an imperfect representation. The true form is present in Jesus Christ.[11] These things were not the image, but the shadow. Seeing that they only served to illustrate the truth of Jesus, the sacrifices

---

[11] Thompson, 129.

made under this law could never permanently take away the sin debt.

Even though these sacrifices were offered often, they could not completely satisfy. That such offerings were made "year by year" on the annual Day of Atonement only proved that they could never make "the ones coming thereunto perfect." If they could have taken away the sin debt *"then would they not have ceased to be offered? For the worshipers, once purified, would have had no more consciousness of sins"* **(10:2).** If these sacrifices could make the worshippers perfect, they would have ceased as a one-time offering would have sufficed, and they would have had "no more consciousness of sins." But they were continuing to be offered as *"in those sacrifices there is a reminder of sins every year. For it is not possible that the blood of bulls and goats could take away sins"* **(10:3-4).**

The offerings under the law were never intended to provide complete atonement, but only to serve as a yearly reminder of a person's sin debt to God. Complete forgiveness through those sacrifices and offerings was never the point behind them. The sacrifices under the law served to prefigure the sacrifice of Christ by teaching them of the need of sacrifice and to appreciate giving their first fruits to the Lord, just

169

as God would soon give the best of heaven for them. The law was intentionally designed by God to be weak and faulty and not to cleanse the conscience. God never intended the law to be permanent or for its sacrifices to be a permanent means of atonement.

"Therefore, when He came into the world, He said: Sacrifice and offering You did not desire, But a body You have prepared for Me. In burnt offerings and sacrifices for sin You had no pleasure" (10:5-6). In verses 5-7 the writer cites Psalms 40:6-8 to teach that even the OT itself rejected the idea of such offerings and sacrifices being sufficient to take away sin (see also Isaiah 1:11 and Micah 6:6). David was prophesying of Christ coming to do the will of His Father, because such offerings were insufficient. It is interesting to note that the writer has already given us a reference in which the Father referred to the Son as "God" (Hebrews 1:8-9), and now he provides a reference in which the Son refers to the Father as God. Observe, *"Then I said, 'Behold, I have come— In the volume of the book it is written of Me—To do Your will, O God...'"* (10:7-10).

In Hebrews 10:8-10, we have what can be considered a divine commentary of Psalms 40:6-8. The writer clearly states that he had to take away the first to establish the second. One could not be true to both covenants at the same time (see Romans 7:1-6). The readers must choose whether to go back to the old covenant (in which there is no atonement, redemption, or promise) or devote themselves to the law of Christ. It was (and remains) either the first or the second – not both (Galatians 5:4). Remember, it was by the will of God that He took away the first so that He might establish the second (cf. Hebrews 8:7, 13). And "By that will we have been sanctified through the offering of the body of Jesus Christ once for all" (10:11).

It is by the offering of Christ that we are sanctified (set apart for a holy purpose) from the world. Sanctification is accomplished when we obey the gospel and become a Christian (John 17:17; Ephesians 5:26). It is made possible through the offering of His body "once for all." The phrase "once for all" contrasts the sacrifice of Christ to the sacrifices of the old law which could not be made once and for all. Under the law, those sacrifices had to be offered continually, year after year, because they could never fully take way sins. However, the blood of Jesus was offered once for all because His blood completely and totally washes away our sins and fulfills the promise of God that "Their sins and iniquities I will remember no more."

"And every priest stands ministering daily and offering repeatedly the same sacrifices, which can never take away sins" **(10:11).** Here we find another verse which seems to indicate the temple was still standing in Jerusalem at the time of writing. The Israelites offered sacrifices not just yearly, but daily. They had a daily reminder of their sin debt. Their priests stood daily offering the same insufficient sacrifices which could never take away sins. While the priests may have been sincere in their ministry, the sacrifices they offered were invalid.

"But this Man, after He had offered one sacrifice for sins forever, sat down at the right hand of God, from that time waiting till His enemies are made His footstool" **(10:12-13).** No priest that had ever lived could make this claim. *Jesus is not standing* offering daily sacrifices. He offered one perfect, complete, all-sufficient sacrifice, for every soul that will ever live, perfect enough to cleanse every sin ever committed, and *sat down* at the right hand of the throne of God signifying to us His redemptive work is finished. *"For by one offering He has perfected forever those who are being sanctified"* **(10:14).** Now the comparison is

completed between Christ's priesthood and that of the Israelites.

"But the Holy Spirit also witnesses to us; for after He had said before, 'This is the covenant that I will make...'" **(10:15-18).** The writer again cites Jeremiah's prophecy to emphasize that this promise has been kept and now in Christ Jesus "there is no more offering for sin." In Hebrews 8:8-12, Jeremiah 31:31-34 was quoted to prove the old law was now obsolete, it is quoted again here to establish the permanence of the era of perfection inaugurated under Christ and His new covenant.[12]

Summary

The world will never have another Jesus. If He is rejected, all hope of salvation is rejected. He is the one and only Savior of the world. We will never have another Savior. If we have Him, we will never need another Savior.

Just imagine how many sins have been committed in the lives of the billions of people who have lived upon this earth. If this world stands for a billion years from now how many sins will be committed? Yet, this one sacrifice of Jesus Christ is so great and so perfect that by its efficacy God has

---

[12] Bruce, 242.

said, "I will remember their sins no more." He only had to offer His sacrifice once. His blood takes the sin debt away forever. His blood cleanses our hearts and purifies our conscience. Truly this has been written upon the hearts and in the minds of all who love Him. His sacrifice will forever stand as the single greatest event ever to occur in this world's vast history. How truly wonderful is Jesus Christ, "which is, and which was, and which is to come, the Almighty" (Revelation 1:8).

Section Five
The Application of the Truths Discussed
10:19 – 12:29

"Therefore, brethren, having boldness to enter the Holiest by the blood of Jesus, by a new and living way which He consecrated for us, through the veil, that is, His flesh, and having a High Priest over the house of God..." **(10:19-21).** Here we have a summary statement for the book of Hebrews up to this point. Through Christ's sacrifice we have (1) boldness to enter the holiest to approach God's throne; (2) a new and living way. Not just new, but new *and living* way, which is our covenant with God; and (3) Christ as our High Priest over the house of God. The prayers of Christians now ascend before His throne as a sweet-smelling aroma (Revelation 8:3).

"...let us draw near with a true heart in full assurance of faith, having our hearts sprinkled from an evil conscience and our bodies washed with pure water" **(10:22).** Having the summary of the book in mind, three "let us" exhortations are given in succession to produce an application of the principles taught in the homily. By saying "let us" the

writer of Hebrews informs us that we have the power or capability to do what he is asking. Let us draw near to God. How? He stipulates: (1) with a true heart; (2) in full assurance of faith; and (3) by being free from an evil conscience.

The first exhortation is to draw near with a true heart. The scriptures are filled with accounts of men and women obeying and disobeying God. In every instance of obedience, we will find a person obeying God from his heart and from God's word. In every instance of disobedience, we find a person doing *other than*, *more than*, or *less than* what God has commanded. Sometimes their hearts were sincere and sometimes they were not.

The church in Thessalonica received the word of God in the right way, with a true heart. Note: "For this reason we also thank God without ceasing, because when you received the word of God which you heard from us, you welcomed it not as the word of men, but as it is in truth, the word of God, which also effectively works in you who believe" (1 Thessalonians 2:13). We must receive the word of God with the same characteristic of a welcoming heart.

We must draw near to God with full assurance of faith. Such wholehearted conviction can only come when one's faith is established on the promises of God and grounded in the truth of His word. The writer has mentioned the heart of the believer. Now he is alluding to the source of the belief. "A faith that is not grounded on true biblical doctrine is only superstition based in ignorance."[1] To obey the gospel faithfully, we must obey the doctrine of Christ from the heart. Paul wrote to the Romans, "But God be thanked that though you were slaves of sin, yet *you obeyed from the heart that form of doctrine* to which you were delivered. And having been (then, KJV) set free from sin, you became slaves of righteousness" (Romans 6:17-18). When we obey the gospel from the heart and from the Bible, we are set free from sin and become the servants of righteousness.

Commentators have offered various opinions for the significance of the statement, *"having our hearts sprinkled from an evil conscience, and our bodies washed with pure water."* Some theologians have attempted to use this passage as an endorsement of sprinkling and pouring as a mode for baptism. However, if the Bible student will keep this statement in the context of what has already been stated pertain-

---

[1] Martel Pace, *Hebrews* in the Truth for Today Commentary Series (Searcy, AR: Resource Publications, 2007), 423.

ing to consecration under the old law (Hebrews 9:10, 21; Exodus 24:8), no problems should arise in explaining the text. Not only is it another example of an OT statute being used to illustrate a NT truth, but it is also a fulfillment of a promise God made to Israel when they were in captivity. God spoke through His prophet Ezekiel concerning the sprinkling of the conscience, promising Israel, "For I will take you from among the nations, gather you out of all countries, and bring you into your own land. Then I will sprinkle clean water on you, and you shall be clean; I will cleanse you from all your filthiness and from all your idols. I will give you a new heart and put a new spirit within you; I will take the heart of stone out of your flesh and give you a heart of flesh. I will put My Spirit within you and cause you to walk in My statutes, and you will keep My judgments and do them" (Ezekiel 36:24-27).

Israelites were the first to hear the gospel of Christ and to receive a cleansing of conscience and new heart. The church began in Jerusalem and has expanded throughout the world. The church consists of consecrated ones. The "sprinkling" of the blood of Christ has consecrated the church and given us freedom from an evil conscience. While the offerings under the law could not clear the conscience (Hebrews 9:9), the offering of Christ does as the heart is sprinkled and the body is washed.

While various washings were necessary under the old law, only one washing is necessary in the NT – baptism in water for the forgiveness of sin (Acts 2:38). There is "one baptism" required and recognized by God (Ephesians 4:5).

At baptism, sins are washed away (Acts 22:16). Our bodies are washed with pure water. Pure water is stated in connection with the true heart and the clean conscience. A person's baptism is pure when it is done with a good conscience and from the word of God (1 Peter 3:21; Romans 6:3-4, 17). The conscience is touched by the preaching of the gospel (Mark 16:15-16; Acts 2:37) and at baptism this person is sanctified and cleansed through the washing of water by the word (Ephesians 5:26). Baptism is thus a "washing of regeneration" and renewing of the Holy Spirit (Titus 3:5) as the recipient is born again by water and Spirit (John 3:3-5).

"Let us hold fast the confession of our hope without wavering, for He who promised is faithful" **(10:23).** The second "let us" exhortation admonishes us to "hold fast." Hold fast to our confession of hope without wavering, knowing that "He who promised is faithful."

The readers truly had no need to waver. The promises made to them were made by the faithful God, who cannot lie (Titus 1:2), and who swore by Himself. His word stood as their all-sufficient source of hope (Hebrews 6:13-19). God was to be the basis of their confidence. Christ was ever living to make intercession for them.

As Christians, we can hold fast without wavering in faith because of our conviction in the faithfulness of God. The NT is abundantly clear concerning the faithfulness of God and the faith and trust Christians are to place in Him. Note: "God is faithful, by whom you were called into the fellowship of His Son, Jesus Christ our Lord" (1 Corinthians 1:9). "He who calls you is faithful, who also will do it" (1 Thessalonians 5:24).

Again, "If we are faithless, He remains faithful; He cannot deny Himself" (2 Timothy 2:13). "If we confess our sins, He is faithful and just to forgive us our sins and to cleanse us from all unrighteousness" (1 John 1:9).

Moreover, "the Lord is faithful, who will establish you and guard you from the evil one" (2 Thessalonians 3:3). And, "God is faithful, who will not allow you to be tempted beyond what you are able, but with the temptation will also make the way of escape, that you may be able to bear it" (1 Corinthians 10:13).

Now we read in this text of Hebrews, "Let us hold fast the confession of our hope without wavering, for He who promised is faithful" (Hebrews 10:23). Therefore, the readers should do as Peter exhorted and, "let those who suffer according to the will of God commit their souls to Him in doing good, as to a faithful Creator" (1 Peter 4:19).

The third and final "let us" exhortation of this passage is found in v. 24. ***"And let us consider one another in order to stir up love and good works…" (10:24).*** The exhortation involves consideration of our brethren to encourage them to love and good works. A person can instill courage or take courage from another. The writer teaches us to encourage one another to love and good works. Of course, this begins with a proper consideration of one another. Note, "consider one another…" We are to consider our brethren and how we might encourage them and vice versa. We should consider and appreciate how much of the NT is written to encourage brethren to be faithful, continue faithfully, or repent of unfaithfulness. However, such encouragement cannot be provided to someone who is not in contact with his brethren or hearing the preaching of the gospel.

Therefore, Christian must refrain from *"forsaking the assembling of ourselves together, as is the manner of some, but exhorting one another, and so much the more as you see the Day approaching"* **(10:25).** It is hard to encourage a brother who is never or seldom seen. The assembly of the church into one place seems to be the clear meaning of the phrase (see 1 Corinthians 11:17ff.). The church is an assembly of people who have been called out of sin and assembled in the spiritual body and kingdom of Christ (Colossians 1:13). The assembly assembles on the first day of the week (Acts 20:7).

Concerning the day approaching, one view to be considered is that it is the Lord's Day (Revelation 1:10), the day on which He was resurrected (Luke 24:1), the day on which the church assembles (Acts 20:7) – the first day of the week. As the church sees this day approaching, we should be found encouraging one another to assemble, rather than forsaking our fellowship in Christ.[2] To forsake the assembly would be to sin willfully (v.26).

---

[2] In his commentary, David McClister offers four possible explanations for the day that is approaching, none of which is the first day of the week. His possible interpretations are (1) the day of judgment; (2) the day of the destruction of Jerusalem; (3) the day of persecution; (4) the day of spiritual growth for the church. McClister, 360-61.

A second plausible view is that the day is the day of our Lord's return and final judgment. Christians should certainly view this day as one that is approaching. Paul encouraged the church at Thessalonica and other places concerning the coming day of Christ (1 Thessalonians 5:1ff.). It is not beyond reason that this could be the day in mind for the writer of Hebrews. If this is the case, the writer would be encouraging his readers not to forsake the Lord's Day assembly, and to continue encouraging faithfulness in each other as the coming day of the Lord is approaching.

"For if we sin willfully after we have received the knowledge of the truth, there no longer remains a sacrifice for sins..." **(10:26).** The meaning from the verb tense in this passage is, "if we go on sinning willfully" or "continue sinning willfully," there no longer remains a sacrifice for sins. The meaning of this statement must be considered for two significant reasons.

In the first place, as the writer has proven, there will never be another sacrifice for sin to replace the sacrifice of Christ (ch.9-10). His sacrifice is *the* one and final offering for sin. If we reject His atonement, we reject all hope for the forgiveness of sins. But this is not the only lesson to be imparted from the statement. For If we continue sinning willfully, the blood of Christ no longer remains for us as a source of cleansing and forgiveness. Through continuous deliberate sin, all blessings found in Him are ultimately forsaken by the sinner (cf. 2:1-3; 3:12-13; 6:4-6).

Once more, the writer is warning his readers about the possibility and consequences of apostasy. The writer will soon state that the willful sin is tantamount to trampling Jesus beneath the feet, despising the blood of the covenant as a common thing, and insulting the Spirit of grace (10:29). If the apostate brother remains in this condition, spiritual renewal will be impossible (6:4-6). His sin will become a "sin unto death" (1 John 5:16).

Without forgiveness, what does remain for the rebellious Christian? The writer states, *"...but a certain fearful expectation of judgment, and fiery indignation which will devour the adversaries"* **(10:27).** Christians who have forsaken the Lord to return to a life characterized by willful sin have no longer any hope or boldness in judgment (1 John 4:17). It cannot be said that they would love His appearing (2 Timothy 4:8). Heaven does not await them, only a certain fearful expectation of the judgment and of fiery indignation which shall consume the adversaries of God.

Attempts to deny the force of the passage and the apostasy in view are plenteous among evangelical commentators of the text. It is asserted that such ones merely professed faith in Christ but were never true believers. However, the people under consideration had been sanctified by the blood of the covenant of Christ and were trampling it beneath their feet.

The writer further explains this point by way of an OT illustration. *"Anyone who has rejected Moses' law dies without mercy..."* **(10:28-29)** According to the Law of Moses, the person sentenced of a transgression worthy of death according to the testimony of at least two witnesses was sentenced to die without mercy. The writer now asks, of how much *worse punishment* will he be thought worthy, who has (1) trampled the Son of God underfoot, and (2) counted the blood of the covenant, by which he was sanctified, a common (unholy, KJV) thing, and (3) insulted the Spirit of grace?

To say this person was never saved is a futile attempt to justify the "once saved always saved" doctrine, for this person had been sanctified by the blood of Christ. The NT teaches plainly that a Christian must continue believing, repenting of sin, and obeying the Lord. The terms of the covenant do not end when the covenant is entered, they begin.

185

The manner of life for a Christian should be characterized by holiness and godliness (2 Peter 3:11), growing in the grace and knowledge of the Lord (2 Peter 3:18), maturing in Christ (Hebrews 5:11ff.), and fellowship with the saints (Hebrews 10:24-25).

As we have learned from Hebrews already, it is possible to depart from the living God through the deceitfulness of sin (Hebrews 3:12-13). If this happens, God has provided a way to be *restored* (Galatians 6:1-2) and *converted* (James 5:19-20) to the faith. The erring Christian must remember, repent, and return. "Remember therefore from where you have fallen; repent and do the first works" (Revelation 2:5).

"For we know Him who said, 'Vengeance is Mine, I will repay...'" (10:30-31). The writer concludes his line of reasoning by bringing our attention to the very nature of God. God's justice demands retribution for sins. He has paid retribution for us through His Son. If we choose to turn our back to the offering of Christ, then we must pay the personal retribution and punishment that we owe.

God will repay the wicked for their iniquity (cf. Deuteronomy 32:35-36). God will not acquit the wicked (Nahum 1:3). He will reward or recompense for the good or the evil we have done (see 2 Corinthians 5:10). The only way a sinner can stand justified on the judgment day is to be cleansed by Christ's blood in this life, while salvation and mercy avail. If Christ is forsaken, wayward Christians must be reminded that death will come, and punishment will be brought to fruition. *"For we know Him who said, 'Vengeance is Mine, I will repay,' says the Lord. And again, 'The Lord will judge His people.' It is a fearful thing to fall into the hands of the living God."*

"But recall the former days..." **(10:32-34).** Evidently, these brethren had already been enduring some persecutions. After their conversion, they had suffered reproaches and afflictions, and had been companions of those who had suffered the same. The writer also indicates that he had at one time been in chains. It is also possible that he was again/still imprisoned at the time of this writing (see Hebrews 13:19).

Two forms of persecution which they had been called to suffer are mentioned. One was imprisonment; the second was economical. Notice how they *joyfully accepted the plundering of your goods.* A third form of persecution and the most severe, which was the shedding of blood, remained to be seen (Hebrews 12:4).

The writer encourages these Christians to endure persecution by looking ahead. The Christian religion is a forward-looking religion (see Luke 9:62). If these brethren would continue looking ahead to heaven as an enduring substance (cf. Matthew 6:19-21), they would be able to endure persecution and keep their faith. It was only when they began to look back with longing eyes upon their past freedom from persecution that they became doubtful in faith, drained of hope, and in danger of apostasy.

"Therefore do not cast away your confidence, which has great reward..." **(10:35-38).** Just as trampling Christ's blood beneath one's feet carries with it a worse punishment, keeping the faith through trials and tribulations brings a great reward. "Therefore, consider the goodness and severity of God: on those who fell, severity; but toward you, goodness, if you continue in His goodness. Otherwise, you also will be cut off" (Romans 11:22).

Also note *when* one receives the promise of his inheritance. The writer says, *"after you have done the will of God."* The student of the Bible will find this to be true of all spiritual blessings in this life and for the blessing of heaven eternal. Compare what is being said at this point in the homily with what was said previously concerning Abraham

(6:15). In both passages (ch. 10 and ch. 6), a warning concerning apostasy is made and then an encouragement to endure is offered. The encouragement in both cases included reminders of God's promises and that those promises become reality after His word is kept.

"But we are not of those who draw back to perdition, but of those who believe to the saving of the soul" (10:39). Couched within a warm vote of confidence for the readers, we have a short statement summarizing what it means to live by faith. No matter how severe the persecution or suffering may be, it is only "for a little while." Despite these things, *"we,"* the writer affirms, believe even unto the saving of the soul.

Hebrews 10 concludes with the writer expressing his confidence that his readers were not "of them that draw back unto perdition," as he warned in the latter part of that chapter (10:26ff.), but rather these people were "of them that believe to the saving of the soul." Remember also that the writer quoted from Habakkuk, saying, "the just shall live by faith" (Habakkuk 2:4). Chapter eleven will begin by giving a definition of the faith these brethren had and were called upon to manifest in daily life.

In Hebrews 11, we will also learn what it means to live by faith through examples of OT history provided to illustrate the virtuous life. From this "Hall of Fame of Faith" the reader will be reminded that such faithfulness is essential to happiness on earth and a heavenly reward.

"Now faith is the substance of things hoped for, the evidence of things not seen. For by it the elders obtained a good testimony" **(11:1-2).** The Christian's faith is based on knowledge, not just any knowledge, but knowledge of God's word (Romans 10:17). The Bible compels us to "prove all things and hold fast to that which is good" (1 Thessalonians 5:21). We do so by searching the scriptures (John 5:39; Acts 17:11) and handling accurately the word of truth (2 Timothy 2:15).

Faith is substantial. Faith is literally the sub-stance – that which stands under or supports – our hope of heaven. Faith is not only *the substance of things hoped for,* but also *the evidence of things not seen.* Because of faith that is based on our knowledge of the word of God, unseen things like God Himself, heaven eternal, and our immortal soul become realities.

Next, the writer expounds upon this definition by briefly reaching back into their heritage and reminding them that it was by this faith that their elders obtained a good report (v.2). The word "elders" in this case should be considered in view of the very broad spectrum of Hebrew history – "the people of old" (NASB). The writer does not have one single event or person in mind, but seemingly the entire history of the OT, and in this chapter, he will remind his readers of some of these men and women who obtained this good report. The elders are the patriarchs and examples of faith which were so deservingly cherished by their descendants and the good report given is the report found in the annals of sacred writ.

"By faith we understand that the worlds were framed by the word of God, so that the things which are seen were not made of things which are visible" (11:3). True, biblical faith leads to understanding God and His works. Through faith derived from the word of God, we understand that the worlds were framed by His word.

God literally spoke the universe into existence (Genesis 1:3ff.). As Christians, we should see no need in alternate theories for creation. Our faith in God and His word is sufficient to understand His creative power. In many cases, scientific hypotheses are not even agreed upon within the scientific community. Many times, scientists change their minds as they uncover new evidence. The Bible, to the contrary, has withstood the test of time. It does not change. When previous scientific thoughts have been forgotten, the Bible has remained true.

The Theory of Evolution states that the origin of life began 3.6-3.8 billion years ago and gradually "unfolded" into the species of life that now exists. The culmination of this unfolding is the species of *Homo sapiens*.

Attempts to compromise are evident with the ideas concerning theistic evolution. To believe the atheistic, evolutionist view of creation is certainly a denial of one's faith. But with theistic evolution, many feel that they can have the best of both worlds. Theistic evolutionists believe that a creator started the evolutionary process.

The Bible reveals that the earth was created in six, 24-hour days. The Gap Theory suggests that a huge "gap" in time exists between verses one and two of Genesis chapter one. During this supposed "gap" there lived successive generations of plants, animals, and even pre-Adamic men. The generation of men is said to have been a perfect generation that was made imperfect through the sin of Satan. Satan supposedly rebelled and brought warfare against God during this period, and as a result, God victoriously destroyed the original creation, leaving the earth in a state of darkness and death. Genesis 1:3 would then be a depiction, not of the original creation, but of a re-creation of the earth in six, 24-hour days.

The Day-Age Theory suggests that the days of Genesis were each long periods of time (ages if you will) and not literal 24-hour days. Hear what the Lord said to Moses at Mt. Sinai, "For in six days the LORD made the heavens and the earth, the sea, and all that is in them, and rested the seventh day..." (Exodus 20:11).

The Bible will always remain the only completely authoritative source about creation. If we cannot trust the Bible on this issue, then who is to say we can trust it on any issue. As in any other matter pertaining to things eternal, we must allow God's word to stand as truth (John 17:17).

"By faith Abel offered to God a more excellent sacrifice than Cain..." **(11:4).** The writer now teaches how a true, biblical faith will lead to worship and sacrifices which

are pleasing to God. Through faith Abel offered a more excellent sacrifice than Cain. Again, we must consider the source of faith in the context of this verse. Abel offered by faith. Cain's offer was rejected because he did not offer by faith. Nadab and Abihu committed sin in this way (Leviticus 10). God will not accept every type of worship (Mark 7:7; John 4:24; Hebrews 9:1). It must be by faith.

"By faith Enoch..." **(11:5).** Verse five presents to us a *walking faith.* Enoch did not experience death as would a normal man (cf. Hebrews 9:27). He was granted this special honor because he "walked with God" (Genesis 5:24). We are instructed several times in the NT how we are to walk (e.g., Ephesians 4:17ff.). When a Bible writer uses the term "walk" in this metaphorical sense, he is referring to our manner of life. One walks with God when he allows Him to direct his steps (Jeremiah 10:23), thus walking in the old paths wherein is the good way (Jeremiah 6:16). It is not for us to direct these steps, but to walk in the light of His word (Psalm 119:105; 1 John 1:7),

"But without faith it is impossible to please Him, for he who comes to God must believe that He is, and that He is a rewarder of those who diligently seek Him" **(11:6).** If we desire to please God in the manner which Enoch exemplifies,

we must have faith. Without faith it is impossible to please God. The implication is clear, one can please God or *never* please God. One cannot please God without (1) believing that He exists and (2) believing that He rewards. God is and God rewards.

He rewards those who diligently seek Him. Once again, the virtue of diligence is mentioned by the writer in connection with one's relationship with God. Diligence is required in study and practice to seek God properly. Through diligent effort, God is sought and can be found. "Seek and ye shall find." The means and ways God can be found are through His world (Acts 17:24-28; Romans 1:19-20) and His word (Romans 1:16-17). One can realize the power of the Creator through His natural creation – the world. But one can never realize the saving grace of the Creator without His word.

"By faith Noah…" **(11:7).** Noah's faith was pleasing to God because he had a *working faith.* Noah walked with God (Genesis 6:8-9). He found favor in the eyes of the Lord and diligently worked to do all that the Lord commanded him (Genesis 6:22). Also consider that Noah was a preacher of righteousness (cf. 2 Peter 2:5). For 120 years he labored and warned the people to repent, but they would not. Yet, he did

manage to save his household, which by any standard is a fine accomplishment.

From these three men, Able, Enoch, and Noah we see that a faith that is pleasing to God diligently and faithfully *worships, walks, and works* according to His blessed will.

"By faith Abraham obeyed…" (11:8). With the example of Abraham, we have an *obedient* faith that embraces the promises of God (vv.8-10; Genesis 12:1ff). In this example of faith, God is granting a promise to Abraham, and Abraham must decide whether he will obey the conditions attached to the promise. God promised land for an inheritance. For Abraham to receive the land, he would be required to leave his father's house and live as a sojourner until the time that God would bring him into the land.

For the Christian nothing has changed. God has granted us a better home (John 14:1-3), and better promises (Hebrews 8:6). Yet, we still must obey His blessed will (Acts 5:32), and sojourn through this life, looking ahead to our heavenly inheritance to obtain the promise.

"By faith he dwelt in the land of promise…" (11:9-10). The writer's statement reveals to us the necessity of having a *sojourning faith.* As did Abraham, we too must not grow

too comfortable in this present world. We must pass the time of our sojourning in fear (1 Peter 1:17). As strangers and pilgrims in this world we must abstain from fleshly lusts which war against the soul (1 Peter 2:11).

In verse ten we have revealed to us the attitude that enabled Abraham to sojourn in such a faithful way – *"for he waited for the city which has foundations, whose builder and maker is God."* Abraham kept his focus on God as the Creator and Ruler of this world and the world to come.

"By faith Sarah..." **(11:11).** In verses 11-12 we see that a *sustaining faith* embraces the promises of God. In Genesis 18:9-15 we learn of the promise that was given to Sarah concerning the son she was to bear. Quite interesting is the fact that the writer considers the entire story of Isaac's birth, and thus includes Genesis 21:1-7 in his brief summary of Sarah's faith. Being old in age, she received the physical strength she so desperately needed to bear a child. She was granted this strength through her faith and trust in God. The laughter that was out of place in Genesis 18 became laughter of joy in Genesis 21.

As Christians we must have this type of faith. We too must have a sustaining faith. We must believe that our Father can cause the impossible to become possible (Matthew 19:26). The child of God can be strengthened through faith in Christ, knowing that he can do all things through Christ which strengthens him (Philippians 4:13).

"Therefore from one man, and him as good as dead, were born as many as the stars of the sky in multitude—innumerable as the sand which is by the seashore" **(11:12).** From Abraham (one man), and he being in his extremely old age (as good as dead), were born as many as the stars and the sand (referring to the greatness of his family). Abraham has left for us a magnificent example of faith. He is called our father and the Friend of God (James 2:21, 23). Abraham is our father in the faith, lineage, and in respect to the promise of God (cf. Romans 4:16ff.). Jesus Christ came through the lineage of Abraham (Genesis 12:3; Galatians 3:16). We are children of God through faith in Christ Jesus (Galatians 3:26-27). "And if ye be Christ's, then are ye Abraham's seed, and heirs according to the promise" (Galatians 3:29, KJV).

Abraham lived his life as a "Friend of God." The relationship between God and Abraham can be oversimplified. The

Lord spoke and Abraham obeyed. Abraham left his country, his family, and his home (Genesis 12:1) and sojourned – not knowing where he was going – for several hundred miles. He did so because he believed God (Romans 4:3, 17). He acted by faith (Hebrews 11:8-9).

God wanted Abraham to leave the past behind and look to the future – "I will make..." was His promise. Abraham was required to sojourn by faith, looking for the land of promise. To reach the land of promise and receive the bless-ings God was willing to bestow, Abraham had to hear God's word, believe Him, and obey Him. He had to leave the for-mer things, look ahead to the promises of God – i.e., hope (Romans 4:18), and stay the course. He could not quit mov-ing toward the Promised Land. The application is clear and corresponds on every point for man to live by faith today.

We can also say many good things about the character of Abraham. He loved unity and was unselfish – "Let there be no strife...for we be brethren" (Genesis 13:8). He was will-ing to fight for those he loved (Genesis 14). He was willing to give to God as a faithful steward (Genesis 14:17-24). Abraham made intercession for others (Genesis 17:23-32). He rose early in the morning to do the will of God (Genesis 21:14). Abraham believed that God would provide (Genesis

22:8). Yet, Abraham was not perfect when God called him (cf. Genesis 12:10-20). He had to mature. He did not possess complete understanding of God's will when God called him (cf. Genesis 16; 17:17). He had to learn.

As with any faithful man, the virtues of Abraham can be seen in life and in death. Realizing that death was approaching, Abraham made provisions for his son – both physical (Genesis 25:5) and spiritual (Genesis 24; 25:11). And, when he died, he was gathered unto his people. We must give thought to such matters as well. How do we plan to die? Are we providing spiritual blessings for our children? Will God continue to bless them after we are gone? To what people shall we be gathered at death?

"These all died in faith, not having received the promises…" (11:13-16). In this passage, we find a comparison of what *was* and what *now is* concerning the promises of God. Those of old, who had not received the fruition of God's promise in Christ, were looking ahead by faith to the fulfillment of God's promises. Our heroes of faith did not maintain an attitude of being worldly minded, but passed through this world with the mindset that this world was not their home. In so doing, they are for us an example that is worth following. By such examples, Christians can appreciate and

honor the great value of the thirty-nine books of the Old Testament as sacred volumes written for our learning (Romans 15:4), containing examples of faithfulness, and even unfaithfulness.

"By faith Abraham, when he was tested..." **(11:17-19).** From Abraham we can also learn the value of an *sacrificing faith* (vv.19-20). In Genesis 22:1-19, we learn of Abraham's willingness to offer his son, his only son Isaac. The passage in Hebrews reveals the thoughts of Abraham as he was preparing to offer his son as he was *"**concluding that God was able to raise him up, even from the dead, from which he also received him in a figurative sense.**"* The commandment to sacrifice Isaac not only proved the faith of Abraham but also foreshadowed the cross (cf. John 3:16).

The just examples of Abraham and Sarah illustrate living by faith in a marvelous way to the original readers and to us. From the faith characterized by our ancestors in the faith, we learn the virtues of a walk with God which *sojourns, sustains, and sacrifices.*

"By faith Isaac blessed Jacob and Esau concerning things to come" (11:20). Isaac (Genesis 22:1-19), Jacob (Genesis 48:14-20), and Joseph (Genesis 50:24-26) were each able to influence the coming generations by their faith. Isaac believed God would keep the covenant He made with Abraham, and later himself. Thus, he blessed Jacob and Esau concerning the future. He believed God held the future in His hands. By faith, Isaac pleased God, believing that He rewards those who diligently seek Him. His faith was communicated or *transmitted* to his children and his children's children.

"By faith Jacob, when he was dying, blessed..." (11:21). Jacob, in turn, did the same. Jacob's faith was *transformative*. Faith in God transformed Jacob (Heb. *deceiver*) into Israel (Heb. *prince*). He believed God's promises and offered a blessing to the sons of Joseph.

"By faith Joseph, when he was dying..." (11:22). Joseph knew God promised his family the land of Canaan and made provisions for his burial in that land. He had faith that God would keep His word and that his bones could one day be laid to rest alongside his fathers. Just as his bones were *transferred* from Egypt to the land of promise, his faithful example can be passed down to the readers and to us.

The examples of Isaac, Jacob, and Joseph present to us the benefits of having faith pleasing to God as characterized through its *transmission, transformation, and transference*.

"By faith Moses when he was born..." (11:23). In verses 23-31 we read of the faith of the Jews in the generation of the Exodus. Verse 23 brings to our attention the faith of Moses' parents. Pharaoh became afraid of the rising population of the Jews in his country and ordered every son born of the captive Hebrews to be slain (Exodus 1:7-22). By faith, Moses' mother obeyed God rather than man and spared their son (Exodus 2:1-3).

It seems that this passage reveals a little more to the story from Moses' childhood than we find in Exodus. Herein, we learn how both of his parents were involved in hiding him for three months, while Exodus only speaks of the mother's involvement. By faith they obeyed the law of God by allowing their son to live, rather than yielding to the law of Pharaoh which called for his destruction.

"By faith Moses, when he became of age..." (11:24-29). In verses 24-28, the writer reminds his readers of the faith of Moses. He begins by observing the sacrifice Moses made to live with his people. He could have had a life of luxury and

nobility. He was one of the heirs to the wealth, fortune, and fame that would have come with being a descendant of Pharaoh. Yet, Moses chose to suffer affliction rather than to enjoy the pleasures of sin "for a season" (KJV).

Sin affords no lasting pleasure. Paul once asked, "What fruit had ye in those things, whereof now ye are ashamed" (Romans 6:21, KJV)? Moses "esteemed the reproach of Christ" which is to say that he bore reproach in his time in the likeness that Christ bore for the world. Moses considered such reproach to be greater than all the treasures of Egypt. Just as Moses' parents prioritized the will of God over the will of Pharoah, Moses *prioritized* the riches of heaven above the riches of Egypt. By faith Moses *persevered* (v.27). By faith Moses *put into action* the commandments of God as he obeyed God concerning the Passover (v.28). And, by faith Moses led Israel as they *passed through* the Read Sea on dry ground to witness their enemy being destroyed.

Moses stood at the water's edge with Egypt's army pursuing. All he had was the word God had spoken to him. He did not get scared, doubt, or lose his faith. Rather, he assured his people by saying, "Do not be afraid. Stand still, and see the salvation of the LORD, which He will accomplish for you today. For the Egyptians whom you see today, you shall see again no more forever" (Exodus 14:13).

The vast body of water was divided and congealed on both sides. To make things easier and possible for them to pass, God dried the bottom. Yet, Moses still had to have tremendous faith to go down into that unprecedented valley and cross to the other side.

The crossing of the Red Sea serves yet as another OT illustration of a NT truth. When the children of Israel crossed the Red Sea, they did it by faith, according to the word of God. When a soul decides to become a Christian, he must do it by faith, according to the word of God. After they crossed the Red Sea, their enemy was destroyed with water. After we cross the waters of baptism our enemy – sin – is destroyed. They became sojourners in the wilderness, looking ahead to the land of promise. We are sojourners in this life, looking ahead to our land of promise – heaven. The unfaithful fell in the wilderness. We must take heed and remain faithful so that we do not suffer their fate (cf. 1 Corinthians 10:1-12; Hebrews 2:1-2; Hebrews 3:12ff.).

It seems the initial readers were being tempted to leave the church and some longed for a return to Judaism so that they might be freed from persecution. In Rome, the Jewish religion was recognized by the state, and during this time it was free from any state-enforced persecution. Christianity was not. Therefore, if these Christians would have decided to leave the Lord and return to the law, they would have been freed from any persecution befalling the church.

Thus, they were reminded of Moses' faith which *prioritized* his relationship with God and his eternal destiny, *persevered* the wrath of Pharoah by keeping before him the unseen King, *put into action* the commandments of God pertaining to the Passover, and *passed through* to safety through the only avenue provided by God. In so doing, he and his people were liberated from the tyranny of Pharaoh and the bondage of Egypt. Christians have experienced the reality of this experience when they pass through the one avenue provided by God – Jesus Christ (John 14:6) and are liberated from the tyranny of Satan and the bondage of sin (cf. Romans 6:6-14).

"By faith the walls of Jericho fell down…" **(11:30).** The children of Israel were commanded to march around the city once a day for six days, and on the seventh day they were to march around it seven times (Joshua 6). It was not until *after* they obeyed by faith that the walls fell as God had promised.

"By faith the harlot Rahab..." **(11:31).** In verse 31 we are told of the faith of Rahab (Joshua 2:1-24; 6:22-25). Rahab believed that she and her family would be spared and so she received the spies with peace. *When* she did so, they were spared. The events at Jericho serve to reinforce the message that God's promises are kept *after/when* men obey.

"And what more shall I say? For the time would fail me..." **(11:32-38).** A fitting verse to introduce this section of scripture would be 1 John 5:4, *"For whatever is born of God overcomes the world. And this is the victory that has overcome the world — our faith."* In our hymnals we find a most uplifting spiritual song titled, *Faith is the Victory,* and indeed it is. *Faith* proved to be the deciding factor between victory and defeat for those who overcame the world. In each of these cases we find faith made evident by obedience to the conditions of God.

Hebrews 11:32 lists various champions of faith and verses 33-37 remind us of the great things these champions accomplished. They accomplished such marvelous victories "through faith." By God's grace, Daniel stopped the mouths of lions. Shadrach, Meshach, and Abednego quenched the violence of fire. David escaped the edge of the sword. Samson's strength was restored from weakness. Gideon and

Joshua were valiant in fighting and scattered the armies of aliens. We know Elijah raised a child from the dead. Many other examples could be given that would fit these descriptions. We are also told of the torment and torture that many of these people temporarily faced, and yet how they endured and overcame by faith.

"And all these, having obtained a good testimony through faith, did not receive the promise, God having provided something better for us, that they should not be made perfect apart from us" **(11:39-40).** Even though they did not live to see the fulfillment of God's promises concerning His Son, they left for us a good report. By our accepting Christ and keeping His mission alive, their faith is made perfect.

The readers could and should have learned from such heroic figures of faith. The same God who watched over these OT heroes of faith was watching over the readers of the homily. He is watching over His children today as well.[3]

---

[3] A beautiful and meaningful passage to remember when persecuted is found in Paul's epistle to the Romans. "Who shall separate us from the love of Christ? shall tribulation, or distress, or persecution, or famine, or nakedness, or peril, or sword? As it is written, For thy sake we are killed all the day long; we are accounted as sheep for the slaughter. Nay, in all these things we are more than conquerors through him that loved us. For I am persuaded, that neither death, nor life, nor angels, nor principalities, nor powers, nor things present, nor things to come, Nor height, nor depth, nor any other creature, shall be able to separate us from the love of God, which is in Christ Jesus our Lord" (Romans 8:35-39, KJV).

"Therefore we also, since we are surrounded by so great a cloud of witnesses, let us lay aside every weight, and the sin which so easily ensnares us, and let us run with endurance the race that is set before us" **(12:1).** Let us first notice the thought of being *"surrounded by a great a cloud of witnesses."* Picture a race taking place; participating in it are men like Abraham, Moses, David, and the remaining roll from the previous chapter. Amidst this marathon are the readers and the writer of Hebrews. Also include the great heroes of faith from the NT.

A person can be surrounded by the best possible examples, but if that person never realizes and follows the example set before them, such wonderful examples would be in vain. Upon appreciating the exemplary faithfulness of the great cloud of witnesses, strive to do the same. Upon admiring the way these champions ran and the way they finished, we are provoked to ask, "How can I run as they ran?" The remainder of verse one provides the answer, *"let us lay aside every weight, and the sin which so easily ensnares us..."*

Having observed the proper way to run from great examples of faith, lay aside any unnecessary weight that might burden or hinder running and finishing life's race. Peter also taught the need to lay aside sinful hinderances to faithfulness (cf. 1 Peter 2:1-3).

Sin is the transgressing of God's law (1 John 3:4). Sin is what separates us from God (Isaiah 59:1-2). The writer is illustrating the need for continued repentance in the life of the believer. Repentance certainly involves laying aside sin, and not continuing therein. In plain terms, we should realize what the things are which are causing us to stumble and to become discouraged and learn to avoid them.

Next, notice the exhortation *"and let us run with endurance the race that is set before us."* The race Christians run is a marathon, not a sprint. It requires endurance. After seeing the example set before us, and having determined to lay aside the sin which besets us, finish what you have started (cf. 1 Corinthians 9:24-27). Finish the course (2 Timothy 4:7).

"...looking unto Jesus, the author and finisher of our faith..." (Hebrews 12:2-3). Hebrews 12:2-3 are possibly the most significant to understanding the purpose of the message being delivered. Christ is exalted as the supreme example of faith in this great cloud of witnesses. He is at the beginning and waiting for His people at the finish line. He has finished His race on earth with joy. The "joy" that was set before Christ was not the immediate agony of the cross which He endured, it was the result, it was the finish line. He was looking unto the end, even the salvation of our souls. The result of the cross brought and brings Him joy. Likewise, the readers were not to be focused on their immediate trials, but the end of their faith, their eternal home in heaven.

For the church, the cross serves as the ultimate example of endurance. We too must take up our cross and follow him (Matthew 10:38; 16:24). We look *unto* Jesus. We are looking ahead, looking forward. We consider His example to keep from becoming weary and fainting in our souls or *minds*. Outward demonstrations of our religion are obvious. But, at its core, Christianity is a religion of the heart, soul, and mind. We obey God from the heart (Romans 6:17). "Blessed are the pure in heart…" (Matthew 5:8).

Satan attacks our hearts and minds more than our bodies. If he can overcome our will, he will defeat us. Knowing this, Satan has permeated every facet of society. Paul refers to him as the "god of this world" (2 Cor. 4:4). The world is under his influence (1 John 5:19). How do we keep him from overcoming our minds in this present evil age (Galatians 1:4)? Jesus said, "In your patience possess ye your souls"

(Luke 21:19, KJV). Christians endure hardship by constantly considering Him, *"that endured such hostility from sinners against Himself."*

"You have not yet resisted to bloodshed, striving against sin" **(Hebrews 12:4).** The readers, like us, had need for endurance. The suffering they were experiencing had not yet reached its most severe climax, the shedding of blood. The writer was very concerned with how they were going to face their trials as they intensified.

On two occasions they were told to consider Jesus. The first time it was in connection with the Israelites who fell in the wilderness (chapter 3). This time, it follows the example of those who endured, the greatest being Christ. At this point, they were on the fence, so to speak. They could have gone either way. They could fall like the Israelites did in the wilderness, or they could overcome, like the heroes of faith. The determining factor would prove to be their mindset. Were they strong enough in mind to keep the faith?

"And you have forgotten the exhortation..." **(Hebrews 12:5-6).** Verses 4-11 teach us that we are perfected through endurance and discipline (cf. James 1:2-4; Proverbs 3:11-

12). Christians are admonished (1) not to despise His chastening; and (2) not to faint (quit) when we are chastened. The reasons follow in the forthcoming verses as the thought that will take center stage is the chastisement of the Lord. It is difficult to discern the difference every time between the chastening of the Lord and the various common trials of life. Not every trial we face should be viewed as a chastening from God. For example, Job was tried by the devil. Moreover, some troubles come from our own doing. We reap what we sow in this life for good or evil (Galatians 6:7).

However, it does appear that a connection is being made by the writer regarding trials and chastening. It could be that many of the trials are permitted – not caused – by God in order that we might be strengthened, trained, and educated[4] (see also 1 Corinthians 10:13; James 1:12ff.).

Nevertheless, the point remains that we should not take such things lightly, nor should we become despondent because of them. The writer provides God's motive for such chastisement: *love*. God loves us as a father loves his children. In this passage God is compared to our earthly fathers

---

[4] Thompson provides insight to the Jewish view of suffering and how they commonly believed its purpose to be punishment from God. He also notes that "discipline" can refer to "education" or "training." Thompson, *Hebrews*, 164-65.

just as in Matthew 7:7-11. The process of being perfected occurs with a greater good in mind.

"If you endure chastening, God deals with you as with sons..." **(Hebrews 12:7-11).** Realizing that God loves us, and perfects us through trials, we should strive to endure the chastening. Keep in mind that all of God's children are called upon to endure some measure of chastisement in life. The illustration of a father and his sons only helps us to realize the disciplinary nature of such things. If we can endure the chastening of our mortal fathers who corrected us, and continue loving and honoring them, should we not also be able to endure our heavenly Father's chastening and continue loving and honoring Him?

That God as the *Father of our spirits* refers to our spiritual relationship with Him as our spiritual Father. We have a mortal father-child relationship, and we have a spiritual Father-child relationship. Emphasis is herein being placed upon the spiritual relationship we each have with God.

Our mortal fathers chastened us, "as it seemed necessary to them." Fathers are called upon to discipline their children for the good of the child (see Proverbs 23:13-14). If a mortal father, who is prone to err just like anybody else, can see the need for discipline, why should we not believe that our eternal Father who is supremely wise in all things would not see the need also? Furthermore, "Human parenting may lack wisdom and be limited in its scope. God's parenting, however, is guided by His perfect knowledge of us and concern for the eternal welfare of His children."[5]

We have seen that the *motive* behind chastisement is love. Next, we learn that the *purpose* of chastisement is our **holiness**. God wants us to be holy as He is holy (1 Peter 1:16) and perfect as He is perfect (Matthew 5:48). While chastening never seems beneficial while we are enduring it, the education received does yield a reward if we determine to endure.

"Therefore strengthen the hands which hang down, and the feeble knees, and make straight paths for your feet, so that what is lame may not be dislocated, but rather be healed" (12:12-13). Verses 12-13 present the vivid picture of a wearied runner straightening-up and gaining his second wind. This is what the readers needed to do. They were fainting in the face of persecution and doubting their faith. They needed to catch their wind, straighten up their posture and

---

[5] Peterson, 292.

path, and finish the race. Truly, they needed to realize the trials would pass, and if they remained faithful, they would receive the reward. Jesus was waiting at the finish line to receive them in glory.

In this portion of our study, not only are we reminded of the great heroes of the preceding dispensations, but also the things that God expects from us. *"Pursue peace with all people, and holiness, without which no one will see the Lord..." (12:14-17).* The Christian's role in this world is one of a peacemaker (Matthew 5:9). Our Lord is the "Lord of Peace" (2 Thessalonians 3:16; Romans 15:33, 16:20). "God is not the author of confusion but of peace" (1 Corinthians 14:33). We bring peace to others through the gospel we preach (Romans 10:15; Ephesians 6:15) and by the life we are called to live (Galatians 5:22; Romans 14:17). Christians are not to seek vengeance or cause division. God is in control of all things. Therefore, we are not to be overcome with evil, but to "overcome evil with good" (Romans 12:21).

Christians are to pursue peace (2 Timothy 2:22; 1 Peter 310-12), live peaceably with all men as much as is possible (Romans 12:18), and produce "the fruit of righteousness [which] is sown in peace by those who make peace" (James

3:18). The peace of God can rule our hearts and provide understanding with a wisdom from above (see Colossians 3:15; Philippians 4:6-7).

The writer of Hebrews also tells us to pursue holiness, *"without which no man shall see the Lord."* Take a moment and compare holiness with hypocrisy. Holiness is representing God accurately in this world (Matthew 5:16). Hypocrisy is condemning others for the things we continue to do in our lives (Romans 2:1ff.). Holiness is a true, pure manifestation of the Godhead living in us. Hypocrisy is a doctrine of the devil which seeks the approval of men, while indulging in the works of the flesh. The church must pursue peace and holiness *diligently.*

Also observe that a man can "fail to obtain" (ESV) or "fall short of" (NKJV) the grace of God. God's grace (favor) is extended by His choosing. He longs to save us but is not required to save anyone. By grace, He has offered His Son for our sins. We can choose to accept His gift or reject it. As Christians, we can fail to obtain His grace if we choose to act like the Israelites in the wilderness (Hebrews 3:12-13). We can leave our first love and fall from His grace (Revelation 2:4-5; Galatians 5:4). We can trample His blood beneath our feet and count His covenant as unholy (Hebrews

6:6, 10:29). We must be diligent so that this does not happen to us (cf. 2 Peter 1:5-11).

Why should we live this way and be so diligent? The answer: *"lest any root of bitterness springing up trouble you, and thereby many be defiled"* (KJV). We are called to be at peace and content with what we have. Bitterness is generally associated with envy, malice, and discontentment, all of which are contrary to the Christian faith. One cannot have joy and love and peace and be bitter at the same time, lest he becomes double-minded and unstable in all his ways.

Esau stands as an example of such a bitter person. He was not content with what he had. He wanted something as trivial as a bowl of soup, and for that he sold his birthright. Is there really any difference in Esau and the Christian who sells his soul for "the passing pleasures of sin" (Hebrews 11:25)? When the time came for Esau to receive his inheritance, he wanted to change his mind, but it was too late. On Judgment Day many souls will want to change their minds, but it will be too late. Today is the day of salvation. Now is the accepted time. Just as Esau's crying went unheard, so too will those tears be vainly shed at the Judgment (Matthew 7:21-22; 25:41ff.). Esau should have looked diligently after his birthright when he had the chance, instead of crying about it when it was too late.

"For you have not come to the mountain that may be touched..." **(12:18-24).** Once more, a comparison will be offered between the events from the life of Moses and the blessings extending from the life of Christ. The comparison is made specifically pertaining to the giving of the law through Moses and the giving of the gospel through Christ. The passage vividly presents the scene at Mt. Sinai where Moses received the law (Exodus 19:9-25). It was such a terrible sight that Moses said, "I exceedingly fear and quake." That this mount burned with fire speaks of the volcanic-like activity witnessed coming from the top of the mount (Exodus 20:18; Deuteronomy 4:11; 5:22-26; 9:19; 18:16).

In contrast, verses 21-24 refer to the giving of the law of Christ from Mt. Zion, which is the heavenly Jerusalem (cf. Psalms 48:2; Isaiah 28:16; Revelation 14:1). Notice also how the church and the new covenant are joined in this passage. One cannot have one without the other. The literal Mt. Zion is in Jerusalem. It was in Jerusalem where the church or kingdom of Christ began (Luke 24:46-47; Acts 2:1-4, 47).

The church is referred to here as an assembly, even the "assembly of the first born" (lit. "first born ones"). They are first born ones by virtue of their union with Christ, the Firstborn, and enjoy rights as firstborn sons.

The church is the *ekklesia* or "the called out" of God. The church has been called out of the darkness of sin and ignorance to form the spiritual body and kingdom of Christ.[6] The gospel is the calling to which we should respond obediently.[7] The gospel is the very "voice" of Christ which compels men to follow as His disciples (John 10:27; 8:31-32).

The church is therefore the assembly of the called (Hebrews 12:23). *Ekklesia* is also translated "assembly" in Acts 19:32, 39, and 41. Christians are not called out of our homes and assembled into a theater or town hall but are called out of the darkness of sin and assembled in the spiritual body – the church – of Christ (Ephesians 1:20-23).

The church is now assembled on earth and will someday forever be assembled with Christ in heaven (1 Thessalonians 4:16-18). We can be added to this sacred assembly and spir-

---

[6] cf. Colossians 1:13; 1 Thessalonians 2:12; 1 Peter 2:5, 9-10; 2 Timothy 1:9-10

[7] cf. Romans 1:16; 2 Thessalonians 2:14; Ephesians 3:6

itual kingdom today by hearing the gospel preached (Romans 10:17); believing the facts concerning Christ as revealed in the gospel (John 8:24; 1 Corinthians 15:1-4); turning from the sins which have caused God to turn His face from you (1 Peter 3:12; 2 Peter 3:9); and being baptized into Christ, having called upon His name in a good confession, to wash away our sins (Acts 22:16).

***"See that you do not refuse Him who speaks…"* (12:25-27).** At the beginning of our study, we read that God has in these last days spoken to us by His Son (Hebrews 1:2). We must give a more earnest heed to His words (Hebrews 2:1-4). Throughout Hebrews, we have been reasoning from the significance of that statement. Perhaps Hebrews 12:25 teaches this significant fact as clear as any other passage we have studied. If Moses should have been heard and revered, as God was speaking through him as a servant, and the people could see that, what about the Son of God who speaks from heaven? See that you do not refuse to listen to Christ. "Hear ye Him."

Our Lord is coming *once more* to shake both the earth and the heavens. God used this phrase when speaking through Haggai concerning His judgments on the nations of the earth. (cf. Haggai 2:21ff.). Here, God speaks through the writer of Hebrews using the same terminology with reference to His final act of judgment on the world, which will occur at the return of Christ (cf. 2 Peter 3:10-12). The writer of Hebrews has already affirmed Christ "will appear a second time" (Hebrews 9:28). At His return, Jesus will gather the kingdom of God (Matthew 13:24-30; 36-43) and bring it into its heavenly and eternal fulfillment (Matthew 25:34).

"Therefore, since we are receiving a kingdom which cannot be shaken, let us have grace, by which we may serve God acceptably with reverence and godly fear. For our God is a consuming fire" **(12:28-29).** That which shall remain after His return is that which cannot be shaken – namely, His kingdom. When referencing Daniel 2:44, we see that both passages refer to the same group, which is herein called the "church of the firstborn." The church can be described as a kingdom when referring to its government. Christ is King.[8] Christians live under His rule and His law.

---

[8] The word *kingdom* describes the government of the church. T.W. Brents observed, "As respects law, the church is truly a *kingdom* – an *absolute monarchy*. All its laws emanate from the King, and its subjects have no part in making them. There is no *representative democracy* connected with it. No council, convention, or legislative assembly has power or authority to abolish, alter, or amend them. It is a *kingdom*, not a *republic*." T.W. Brents, *The Gospel Plan of Salvation* (Bowling Green, KY: Guardian of Truth Foundation, 1987), 118.

The writer concludes this portion of the text with a reminder of how Christians should serve and honor God. Every Christian should offer service to God with *reverence* and *godly fear*, for God is a consuming fire. When we combine the words "reverence" and "godly fear" we get one word – *piety*. Just as the word itself is seldom used anymore, piety is virtue seldom seen. Piety was a common theme especially in the sermons of the 17th century Puritan preachers. Should there be revival in the world again, the church will find that "piety" will have once again become a frequent theme for preachers. Revival cannot occur without reverence and godly fear.

Our God is a consuming fire. Perhaps we do not wish to think of God in these terms. However, such strong language should cause earnest self-reflection and repentance if necessary. We must not wait until hell to decide to repent, for it well be too late (cf. Hebrews 12:17). One should not have to experience God's consuming fire to believe it. Let us take the words of the writer seriously as serve God accordingly.

Summary

In this section of Hebrews, we have found exhortations to remain faithful, hold fast, and encourage faithfulness among our brethren. We have been reminded of the grievous consequences of willful sin and apostasy. We have been encouraged to live by faith unto the saving of the soul.

Chapter eleven defined faith for us and illustrated it by calling to our remembrance the great heroes of faith in the OT. Chapter twelve provided the application for living by faith and considering Christ amid the trials we face. If we will look to Him, and consider Him, we will not only find strength to endure, but we can endure by living peaceable, holy, virtuous, and pious lives.

Section Six
The Christian and Life's Relationships
13:1 – 13:19

With this final chapter, we will see the tone of the homily taking on the characteristics of personal correspondence. Hebrews is not unlike many of the NT epistles in that it ends with various exhortations. The gospels also end with exhortations to "go into all the world." You will also observe that many of the exhortations are relationship oriented.

"Let brotherly love continue" **(13:1).** Brotherly love is a mark of true discipleship (John 13:35). It is by our love for and unity with one another that the world can believe that God sent Jesus, His only begotten Son (John 17:21). Brotherly love is an indication of true spiritual life (1 John 3:14).[1]

The Hebrew Christians who originally received this letter had manifested brotherly love in their ministry to God and His saints (Hebrews 6:10), even in their service to the author (Hebrew 10:32-34). The writer is now teaching that the need for brotherly love never diminishes. Brotherly love is just as

---

[1] Often called the "disciple of love," the apostle John has much to say about brotherly love (see 1 John 3:11, 18; 4:7; 4:20).

important today as it was yesterday. Therefore, "Let brotherly love continue." No matter how much brotherly love these brethren had manifested in times past, their love for one another must continue.[2]

True brotherly love is expressed not only to brethren we know personally, but even to brethren we may be meeting for the first time. It should never be said of us that a visiting brother or sister felt unwelcome in the local congregation where we attend. Our hospitality to one another strengthens that spiritual tie that binds and is not only a beautiful way of life, but is commanded by God (see 1 Peter 4:9; 1 John 5:1ff.; Ephesians 4:32; Philippians 3:12-13). Therefore, *"Do not forget to entertain strangers..." (13:2).* The exhortation here is one of hospitality to people we may not know. Indeed, some did entertain angels unaware (cf. Genesis 18:1-8; 19:1-9; Judges 6:11; 13:2). The point of this verse is not that we should expect to entertain angels that literally come our way, but that when practicing hospitality as we should, the benefits are often unexpected and bountiful.[3]

---

[2] Paul shared this sentiment in his writings to both the Thessalonians (1 Thessalonians 4:9-10), and the Philippians (Philippians 1:9). Peter also expressed the need for brotherly love in stating that it should abound (2 Peter 1:7).

[3] Lightfoot, 247.

***"Remember the prisoners..."* (13:3).** The writer next calls his readers to remember those that were being persecuted and imprisoned for their faith at that present time. Most likely this letter was written during the early portion of Nero's persecution of the church. Roman prisoners were not provided with food and clothing. Such provisions came from family and friends.[4] By provided these needs for Christian prisoners, the brethren would indeed be contributing something well-pleasing to God (cf. Philippians 4:18). Also, we must not discount that another way to remember these fellow brethren would have been through prayer (cf. Acts 12:5; Ephesians 6:18-20).

***"Marriage is honorable among all..."* (13:4).** God will judge those who practice fornication and adultery. Both are works of the flesh and those that practice such works shall not inherit the kingdom of God (see Galatians 5:19-21).

Marriage must be held with honor in every case whether the marriage is between Christians, non-Christians, or a Christian and a non-Christian. In Matthew 5:31-32 and 19:9ff., Jesus clearly taught about marriage, divorce, and remarriage. When turning to Romans 7:1-3 we see that the

---

[4] McClister, 492-93.

duration of the marriage law is life-long. Outside of one's relationship to God, the relationship to one's spouse should be considered dearest of all. It is good to marry. "It is not good that man should be alone."

***"Let your conduct be without covetousness..."* (13:5-6).** Here we find an exhortation which applies to our relationship with material things. What we have contrasted in these two verses are the ideas of contentment vs. covetousness. Paul offers the same comparison when instructing Timothy to charge those who are rich (cf. 1 Timothy 6:17-19). Contentment and covetousness are not compatible and can never coexist. As Christians, we should be happy with the providential care that God gives and remain thankful for every gift from His loving hand. True happiness is not found in the pursuit of riches or having everything you want, but in wanting everything that you have. May we learn contentment as the apostle Paul had in Philippians 4:6-12.[5]

***"Remember those who rule over you..."* (13:7).** Hebrews 13:7 and 17 should be studied together as they both apply to the church's relationship to the elders of the local

---

[5] Also read Luke 12:13ff. and 1 Timothy 6:6ff. for greater knowledge of the subject.

church. To ensure faithful nurturing, guidance, and protection for the flock, the Lord gave qualifications and stipulations for shepherd leaders in every congregation (1 Timothy 3:1-7; Titus 1:5-9).[6] Just as Jesus was a constant companion to the twelve disciples, elders are to remain among the flock (1 Thessalonians 5:12; 1 Peter 5:2), caring for, encouraging, and guiding the church. Yet, the shepherd's ongoing challenge is to teach the flock to obey the Lord's commands. Overseers in the church should be men who have "spoken the word" and live exemplary lives of faithfulness to Christ.

In v. 17 we find the admonition continued: *"Obey those who rule over you..."* **(13:17).** Such leadership is a great need in the Lord's church today. Churches need elders who are worthy of hearing and following. By following such faithful men we will be tremendously influenced in our faith and conviction for Christ. As church members, we must take heed that we do not make their job harder than it already is. Elders have a tremendous responsibility and good ones need to be appreciated.

---

[6] The New Testament depicts *elders* (pl.) serving as shepherd leaders within each congregation. See Acts 11:30; 14:23; 15:2, 4, 6, 22, 23; 16:4; 20:17, 28–29; 21:18; Titus 1:5; Heb. 13:7, 17. Elders were also called bishops, presbyters, pastors, shepherds, and overseers depending upon the passage and the given translation of the Bible.

Also consider the charge to *obey* them. On five different occasions Christians are told to obey another human being. Yet, every time a Christian is given this charge it is conditioned upon man's instruction being in harmony with God's instruction. God is the only One we are to obey without exception or exemption. The five occasions we are told to obey men are (1) here in this passage regarding elders, (2) civil government, (3) servants and masters, (4) children and parents, and (5) wives and husbands.

As elders and overseers of the church, the shepherd leader directs the flock and helps the flock to navigate a faithful course in the world, determining direction for the flock while following the lead of the Good Shepherd. As shepherd leaders follow the example of Christ, the church follows them. But, just as Christ did not lead by example *only* (cf. John 14:15; John 15:10), elders are not to lead *only* by example. The flock is commanded to obey and submit to those who are watching over their souls. The elders have been entrusted with "charge" over the flock (1 Thessalonians 5:12). If the shepherd leaders are faithful in communicating the word of God, the flock must obediently follow them as they follow Christ.

The church must not make the elder's work overly difficult through unnecessary squabbling. The true shepherd leader is a servant leader who oversees the flock as a voluntary service to the flock, hoping to protect the sheep from harm. His interest is not in lording over the flock (1 Peter 5:3). He *serves* because it is his desire to serve and to teach those whom he leads to be servants as well.

By serving the flock, the shepherd is imitating the shepherd leadership of Christ (cf. Mark 10:43-45). Shepherd leaders are active participants in the ministry, serving as models of proper behavior and desires. Such leaders are desirous to see their flock involved in the ministry and mission of Christ and to use their talents and abilities to fulfill their respective ministries and thereby bring glory to God.

Shepherds must lead the flock to an environment conducive to encouragement and edification, both individually and collectively. In such an environment spiritual growth will be achieved and numerical growth will occur (cf. Ephesians 4:11ff.). The flock will be safe and multiply. From Father to Son, Son to apostles, apostles to elders, elders must also encourage shepherd leadership among the flock. There is a point to which every Christian is called to provide pastoral care to one another, which is borne out in the numerous "one another" passages of the New Testament.[7]

The mutual edification of the body of Christ consists of love, encouragement, forgiveness, fellowship, teaching, and care. Each of these actions should be considered an aspect of healthy shepherd leadership. Various relationships within the flock will also require direction and guidance to come from one another (see Titus 2:1–8). Each Christian should desire to be a shepherd leader when the situation calls for it, looking unto the example of the elders of the congregation, and ultimately unto Christ as the "Chief Shepherd and Overseer of our souls."

Jesus Christ is the same yesterday, today, and forever (13:8-9). Christ remains the same yesterday, today, and forever. The nature, virtue, and attributes of Christ shall forever remain unchanging. So too shall His word. The readers had faithful elders who were teaching them the truth of God's word and they were charged to follow and obey their instruction.

---

[7] "One Another" passages in the New Testament include: John 13:34, 35; 15:12, 17; Rom. 12:10; 12:16; 13:8; 14:19; 15:14; 16:16; 1 Cor. 16:20; 2 Cor. 13:12; Gal. 5:13; 6:2; Eph. 4:2; 4:25; 4:32; 5:21 Col. 3:9; 3:13; 3:16; 1 Thess. 3:12; 4:9; 4:18; James 4:11; 5:9; 5:16; 1 Pet. 1:22; 3:8, 9; 5:5; 5:14; 1 John 3:11, 23, 4:7, 11, 12; 2 John 5).

Christians cannot to go beyond what is written (1 Corinthians 4:6; 2 John 9-11). "And no wonder! For Satan himself transforms himself into an angel of light. Therefore it is no great thing if his ministers also transform themselves into ministers of righteousness, whose end will be according to their works" (2 Corinthians 11:14-15). Not even an angel from heaven has the authority to add to or to take from the gospel (Galatians 1:6-9).

Therefore: *"Do not be carried about with various and strange doctrines..." (v.9).* Evidently, these brethren were dealing with the matter of dietary laws and what Christians were permitted to eat. If they followed the teachings of Judaizers, they would fall from grace (cf. Galatians 5:4). The church in Rome was also struggling with this issue (Romans 14), as were other congregations (Acts 15:20).

"We have an altar..." **(Hebrews 13:10-16).** The writer is speaking of the altar of Christ – i.e., His sacrifice on the cross. The carcasses that remained after the offering was made were taken outside of the camp and burned (Exodus 29:14). Jesus was crucified outside the city gate of Jerusalem at Calvary.

The church must go beyond the gates, and we do when we "go into all the world" preaching His gospel (Matthew 28:18-20; Mark 16:15-16; Luke 24:46-47). The writer also reminds us of a previous exhortation to remain focused on the goal – that city to come (cf. Revelation 21). As we look for that city, we do not offer sacrifices on an altar, we offer ourselves as living sacrifices (cf. Romans 12:1-2) and the fruit of our lips in spiritual songs and prayer. We sacrifice our time and means by sharing with those in need. Truly, these are the sacrifices with which God is well pleased (James 1:27).

"Pray for us…" **(13:18-19).** In these two verses we find a request for prayer on behalf of the author. By petitioning the recipients to pray, we are inclined to believe that they knew who the letter was from. Concerning the request for prayer, we see the writer's desire to be faithful to God, live honorable lives, and be restored to these brethren that he might encourage them personally.

Consider some things for which the writer did *not* request prayer. He did not request prayer for his health or his wealth. He did not request prayers for his trials (or theirs) to be lifted. His prayer request was purely spiritual in nature, pertaining only to his relationships with God, the world in which he lived, and his future labors for his brethren.

Summary

The Bible teaches us everything we need to know about one thing – man and his relationship to God; and how that one relationship affects all other relationships in life. In this section of Hebrews, the Christian's relationship to his brethren, strangers, spouse, and elders in the church have been discussed.

By so doing, and with remarkable brevity, the writer has outlined some keys to living successfully as Christians amid various trials and temptations. Be diligent to encourage others, watch who you allow to be your teachers and whose doctrine you follow, love your family and friends as you ought, and above all "go forth to Him."

Section Seven
Conclusion
13:20 – 13:25

The final section of the homily includes a benediction for the readers and a brief postscript. Several reasons to believe that Paul was the writer of Hebrews can be deduced from the remaining verses of this chapter. First, Timothy, Paul's son in the faith, was with the penman. Secondly, the writer was in Italy where Paul was imprisoned on two occasions. And thirdly, he closes the letter with the salutation, "grace be with you all," which is seen in all of Paul's epistles.

Also, we have reason to believe this was the church in Rome because those of Italy saluted them. It is hard to imagine this word of encouragement being as meaningful to any other congregation as it would have been to the church in Rome.

"Now the God of peace…make you complete…" (13:20-21). What did God through this inspired writer hope to accomplish through the sermon? He wanted the readers to be *complete in every good work*. The writer simply wanted them to be the type of working Christian that is well pleasing to God. He prayed for two things: (1) that God would bring them to spiritual maturity; and (2) that they would be found doing His will, working that which is well pleasing in His sight.

"And I appeal to you, brethren, bear with the word of exhortation..." (13:22-25). Here the writer beseeches them to "bear with" or allow the word to have its desired effect. Even the best preaching will be of no avail unless it is received by the hearer.

The sermon was now in their hands. What would they do with it? How would they receive it? Likewise, this little study of the great book of Hebrews is now in your hands. It has been a joy to share this material with you. May God bless and keep you is my prayer!

Bibliography

Allen, David L. *Hebrews*. New American Commentary 35. Nashville, TN: B&H, 2010.

Attridge, Harold W. "Epistle to the Hebrews." Pages 97-104 in vol. 3 of *Anchor Bible Dictionary*. Edited by David Noel Freedman. 6 vols. New York: Doubleday, 1992.

Beasley-Murray, G. R. *The Book of Revelation* in The New Century Bible Commentary, rev. ed. Grand Rapids, MI: Eerdmans,1978.

Boatman, Don Earl. *Helps from Hebrews* in the Bible Study Textbook Series. Joplin, MO: College Press, 1960.

Brents, T.W. *The Gospel Plan of Salvation*. Bowling Green, KY: Guardian of Truth Foundation, 1987.

Bruce, F.F. *The Epistle to the Hebrews*. New International Commentary of the New Testament. Grand Rapids, MI: Eerdmans, 1977.

Cargill, Robert L. *Understanding the Book of Hebrews*. Nashville, TN: Broadman Press, 1967.

Carson, D.A., and Douglas J. Moo. *An Introduction to the New Testament*. Grand Rapids, MI: Zondervan, 2005.

Coffman, James Burton. *Commentary on Hebrews*. Abilene, TX: ACU Press, 1971.

Comfort, Philip W. *A Commentary on the Manuscripts and Text of the New Testament*. Grand Rapids, MI: Kregal, 2015.

_____. *New Testament Text and Translation Commentary.* Carol Stream, IL: Tyndale, 2008.

Edersheim, Alfred. *The Temple: Its Ministry and Services.* Peabody, MA: Hendrickson Publishers, 1994.

Eusebius, *Ecclesiastical History.* (Online)

Harris, R. Laird, Gleason L. Archer, and Bruce Waltke, *Theological Wordbook of the Old Testament.* Chicago, IL: Moody Publishers, 1980.

Henry, Matthew. *Matthew Henry's Commentary on the Whole Bible* : *Acts to Revelation,* 6. (Peabody, MA: Hendrickson Publishers, 1991), 732.

Hurst, L.D. *The Epistle to the Hebrews: Its Background of Thought.* SNTS Monograph Series 65. Cambridge: Cambridge University Press, 2005.

King, Sr., Daniel H. *Hebrews* in the Truth Commentaries. Bowling Green, KY: Guardian of Truth Foundation, 2008.

Kistemaker, Simon. "The Authorship of Hebrews," *Faith and Mission, 18.* 2001.

_____. *Hebrews* in the Baker New Testament Commentaries. Grand Rapids, MI: Baker, 1984.

Laansma, Jon C. "The Book of Hebrews." Pages 274-281 in *The Dictionary for Theological Interpretation of the Bible.* Edited by Kevin J. Vanhoozer. Grand Rapids, MI: Baker, 2005.

Lane, William L. *Hebrews 1-8*. World Biblical Commentary 47A. Dallas: TX: Word, 1991.

Lightfoot, Neil R. *Jesus Christ Today: A Commentary on the Book of Hebrews*. Abilene, TX: Bible Guides, 2001.

McClister, David. *A Commentary on Hebrews*. Temple Terrace, FL: Florida College, 2010.

Metzger, Bruce. *A Textual Commentary on the Greek New Testament*. Second edition. Germany: UBS, 1994.

Milligan, Robert. *A Commentary on the Epistle to the Hebrews* in the Gospel Advocate Commentary Series. Nashville, TN: Gospel Advocate Company, 1989.

Morgan, G. Campbell. *God's Last Word to Man: Studies in Hebrews*. Grand Rapids, MI: Baker Book House, 1974.

Pace, Martel. *Hebrews* in the Truth for Today Commentary Series. Searcy, AR: Resource Publications, 2007.

Peterson, David G. *Hebrews: An Introduction and Commentary* in the Tyndale New Testament Commentaries. Downers Grove, IL: Inter Varsity Press, 2020).

Robertson, A.T. *A Grammar of the Greek New Testament in the Light of Historical Research* Nashville, TN: Broadman, 1934.

_____. *The Epistle to the Hebrews* in Word Pictures in the New Testament 5. Nashville, TN: Sunday School Board of the Southern Baptist Convention, 1932.

Schreiner, Thomas R., and Ardel B. Caneday. *The Race Set Before Us: A Biblical Theology of Perseverance and Assurance.* Downers Grove, IL: Inter Varsity Press, 2001.

Suetonius, *Claudius.* (Online)

Tacitus, *Annals of Imperial Rome.* (Online)

Thayer, Joseph H. *Thayer's Greek-English Lexicon of the New Testament.* Peabody, MA: Hendrickson, 2002.

Thielman, Frank. *Theology of the New Testament: A Canonical and Synthetic Approach.* Grand Rapids, MI: Zondervan, 2005.

Thomas, W.H. Griffith. *Hebrews: A Devotional Commentary.* Grand Rapids, MI: Eerdmans, 1970.

Thompson, James. *The Letter to the Hebrews* in The Living Word Commentaries. Austin, TX: R.B. Sweet, 1971.

Trotter, Andrew H. Jr. *Interpreting the Epistle to the Hebrews.* Guides to New Testament Exegesis 6. Grand Rapids, MI: Baker, 1997.

West, D. Gene. *A Student's Commentary on the Treatise to the Hebrews.* Delight, AR: Gospel Light, 2009.